Tidal power from the Severn Estuary Volume I

REPORT TO

The Secretary of State for Energy

PREPARED BY

The Severn Barrage Committee

LONDON: HER MAJESTY'S STATIONERY OFFICE

© Crown copyright 1981
First published 1981

Energy Papers

This publication is the latest in the Energy Papers series published by the Department of Energy.

The series is primarily intended to create a wider public understanding and discussion of energy matters, though some technical papers may appear in it from time to time.

The papers do not necessarily represent Government or Departmental policy.

Other papers in the series:
Number 1 *United Kingdom oil shales: past and possible future exploitation* (£1.15)

Number 2 *Methane derived alcohols: their use as blending components of petrol* (80p)

Number 3 *Advisory Council on Energy Conservation: Report to the Secretary of State for Energy* (80p)

Number 4 *Energy: the key resource* (43p)

Number 5 *Energy saving: the fuel industries and some large firms* (£1.85)

Number 6 *Advisory Council on Energy Conservation: Paper 1: Policy statement by the Trades Union Congress* (65p)

Number 7 *North Sea costs escalation study* (£4.00)

Number 8 *The Offshore Energy Technology Board: strategy for research and development* (90p)

Number 9 *Geothermal energy: the case for research in the United Kingdom* (£1.85)

Number 10 *Advisory Council on Energy Conservation: Paper 2: Passenger transport: short and medium term considerations* (90p)

Number 11 *Energy research and development in the United Kingdom* (£2.65)

Number 12 *Advisory Council on Energy Conservation: Paper 3: Energy prospects* (£1.10)

Number 13 *National Energy Conference June 22 1976. Vol I Report of proceedings* (£2.30). *Vol II Papers submitted* (£3.25)

Number 14 *Tripartite Energy Consultations February 20 1976* (£1.00)

Number 15 *Advisory Council on Energy Conservation: Paper 4: Industry Group Report Session 1975-76* (£1.20)

Number 16 *Solar energy: its potential contribution within the United Kingdom* (£3.00)

Number 17 *Report of the Working Group on Energy Elasticities* (£2.00)

Number 18 *Advisory Council on Energy Conservation: Paper 5: Road vehicle and engine design: short and medium term energy considerations* (£1.75)

Number 19 *Energy balances: some problems and recent developments* (£1.75)

Number 20 *District heating combined with electricity generation in the United Kingdom* (£3.75)

Number 21 *The prospects for the generation of electricity from wind energy in the United Kingdom* (£2.25)

Number 22 *Energy Policy Review* (£1.75)

Number 23 *Tidal power barrages in the Severn Estuary* (£1.50)

Number 24 *Advisory Council on Energy Conservation: Paper 6: Freight transport: short and medium term considerations* (£1.50)

Number 25 *Advisory Council on Energy Conservation: Paper 7: Report of the Working Group on Buildings* (£1.50)

Number 26 *Advisory Council on Energy Conservation: Paper 8: Energy for Transport* (£1.25)

Number 27 *Severn Barrage Seminar September 7 1977* (£3.25)

Number 28 *Report on research and development 1976-77* (£1.75)

Number 29 *Energy forecasting methodology* (£3.25)

Number 30 *Gas gathering pipeline systems in the North Sea* (£2.50)

Number 31 *Advisory Council on Energy Conservation: Report to the Secretary of State for Energy* (£1.75)

Number 32 *Energy conservation research, development and demonstration* (£2.25)

Number 33 *Energy conservation: scope for new measures and long-term strategy* (£2.00)

Number 34 *Heat loads in British cities* (£2.75)

Number 35 *Combined heat and electrical power generation in the United Kingdom* (£3.75)

Number 36 *Advisory Council on Energy Conservation: Paper 9: Civil aviation: energy considerations* (£2.25)

Number 37 *Advisory Council on Energy Conservation: paper 10: Report on the Publicity and Education Working Group* (£2.00)

Number 38 *Report on research and development 1977-78* (£2.75)

Number 39 *Energy technologies for the United Kingdom Vol I* (£3.00). *Vol II Annexes* (£5.75)

Number 40 *Advisory Council on Energy Conservation: report to the Secretary of State for Energy* (£3.25)

Number 41 *National energy policy* (£1.50)

Number 42 *Wave energy* (£5.00)

Number 43 *Multinational arrangements for the nuclear fuel cycle* (£4.00)

Number 44 *A North Sea gas gathering system* (£6.25)

Number 45 *Prospects for improved fuel economy and fuel flexibility in road vehicles* (£6.20)

Foreword
by the Department of Energy

This document is Volume I of a report prepared by the Severn Barrage Committee. The Committee was set up by the Secretary of State for Energy in 1978 under the chairmanship of Sir Hermann Bondi, to assess the feasibility of a Severn Barrage. This report contains their main findings conclusions and recommendations and these are now under consideration by the Government.

The Department of Energy would like to thank all members of the Severn Barrage Committee for their invaluable work in producing this extensive and detailed report.

Volume II of the report consisting of more technical information for specialist readers will be published separately.

ISBN 0 11 410916 8

Plate 1 Artist's Impression
of the Inner Barrage from Brean Down

NOTE:
The buildings shown near the landfall of the barrage on Brean Down are existing ones. Most were erected as part of the coastal defences during the Second World War but some date back as far as Napoleonic times.

Plate 2: Photographic Simulation, Showing an Aerial View of the Inner Barrage from near Lavernock Point Looking Towards Bridgwater Bay

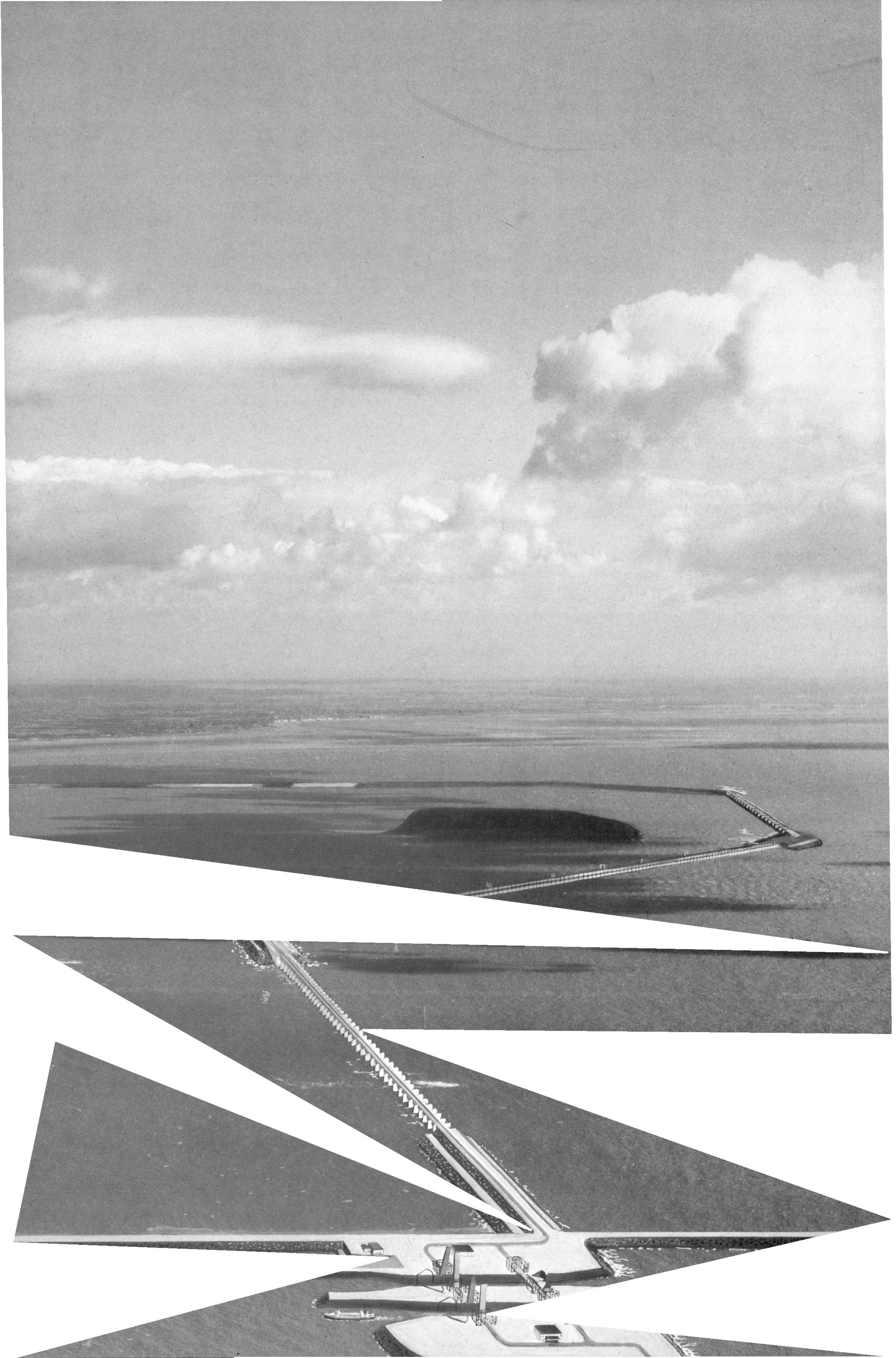

Chairman's Foreword

It is with pleasure that we present this Report on the work done on behalf of our Committee and evaluated by it. Our findings are presented in two volumes. In Volume I we have described our main findings, including some of the problems which have been identified, and have outlined the main arguments which have led to the various conclusions and recommendations. We have tried to write this volume in a manner which should be easy to read for any interested member of the public. Volume II gives a more detailed account of most of the underlying material.

Our report describes the large additions to knowledge that have been gained. These clear some major problems out of the way and clarify those which will need to be resolved by further investigations. The Report lists, we trust comprehensively, the areas of environmental impact and describes the energy and economic considerations which will be relevant to any decision to build the barrage.

If a barrage is to be built, then from the decision to do so to the middle of its operational life would be a period of several decades. No method of analysis can give us a definite answer as to what the world will be like then. Nor can it give a clear answer as to the value of energy at that time or to the future shipping in the Bristol Channel or to public attitudes to the environment, its enjoyment and its protection. The decision to build or not to build must thus always be an act of faith.

I am grateful indeed to all those who have worked so hard against the clock on a problem of immense complexity. This substantial work has been accomplished at a cost of £2.3 million over a period of two and a half years. In particular I want to thank the members of the Committee who gave their time freely and without remuneration and who have always been so well prepared and so ready to follow very complex arguments. I also thank the members and the Chairman of the Working Party on Tidal Power and in particular the Programme Manager who have coordinated this large and enormously varied effort. Finally, special thanks are due to the Secretariat of the Committee who met the many demands on them so cheerfully and effectively.

Sir Hermann Bondi
March 1981

Plate 3: A Severn Barrage Scheme of 1849

The illustration shows a proposal described and drawn by Thomas Fulljames, County Surveyor of Gloucester, for a barrage to be constructed near the site of the Severn Bridge. Its intended purpose was to raise the normal water level behind the barrage to improve shipping access to Gloucester and the inland canal network. The sluices could also be shut against exceptionally high tides to prevent flooding. Transport links across the estuary were also part of the plan, as shown by the railway on top of the barrage and the road immediately underneath.

CONTENTS

VOLUME I   **PAGE**
1. Introduction 1
2. Summary of Findings 3
3. Tides in the Severn Estuary 7
4. Energy Extraction 9
5. Components and Construction of a Barrage 11
6. Technical Feasibility of Estuary Closure 17
7. The Choice of a Barrage Site 19
8. Optimisation of Barrage Components and Operation 21
9. The Option of a Staged Scheme 23
10. The Possibility of a Second Basin for Storage 25
11. The Cost of a Barrage 27
12. The Economics of Tidal Power 31
13. Impacts on Man and the Environment 43
14. Water Levels 45
15. Flow Patterns 47
16. Sedimentation 49
17. Impact on Ports and Shipping 51
18. Recreation and Amenity 55
19. Industrial Impact 59
20. Impact on Sea Defence, Land Drainage and Agriculture 61
21. Impact on Water Quality in the Estuary 65
22. Impact on the Ecosystem and Nature Conservation 69
23. Comparison of Leading Schemes 77
24. The Way Ahead 81
25. Conclusions and Recommendations 85

Annex 1: Terms of Reference of the Severn Barrage Committee 91
Annex 2: Terms of Reference of the Pre-feasibility Study on Tidal Power in the Severn Estuary 92
Annex 3: Role of the Working Party on Tidal Power 93
Annex 4: Organisation and Structure of the Study 95
Annex 5: Definition of Scenarios 98
Annex 6: Criteria for Comparison of Investment in Tidal and Nuclear Power 99
Annex 7: Comparison of Tidal Power with Other Renewable Sources of Energy 101
Annex 8: Visit by the Severn Barrage Committee to the La Rance Barrage, 8th May 1980 103
Annex 9: Glossary of Terms 105

VOLUME 2

1. Data Collection and Analysis
2. Hydraulic Modelling and Sediment Studies
3. Tidal Schemes: Sites, Configurations and Costs
4. Modes of Operation of a Single-basin Scheme
5. Two-basin Energy Storage Schemes
6. Hydro-electric Plant
7. Turbine Caissons
8. Sluice Caissons
9. Embankments
10. Navigation, Ports and Locks
11. Transmission
12. Prototype Trials
13. Economic Evaluation
14. Impacts on the Environment
15. Social and Industrial Implications
16. Recommendations for Future Work
17. Comparison with other Renewable Energy Sources

Plate 4: Artist's Impressions of the Inner Barrage

View from Weston inside the barrage at high tide

View from Lavernock Point outside the barrage at low tide

Introduction 1

The Severn Estuary is one of the world's best sites for tidal power. Moreover it is close to a high capacity integrated electricity supply system. Over many decades numerous schemes for exploiting this energy resource have been put forward, but these have never appeared sufficiently attractive to be investigated in depth. However, the realisation of the last few years that the period of cheap energy is over, and that indeed energy may prove to be a major constraint in future, has lent fresh interest and urgency to the concept of tidal power in general and that of the Severn Estuary in particular.

The current long term power generation strategy is aimed at providing the option of building whatever nuclear stations are required in the 1990's. However, there are doubts about whether a large scale nuclear programme will be possible or acceptable. These doubts arise from public concern over the safety of nuclear power plant and fuel reprocessing procedures, the availability and acceptability of nuclear power station sites and the capacity of the nuclear construction industry to build and commission new plant at the required rate. Also the future cost of nuclear fuel is uncertain and thus the construction of a large nuclear generating capacity may depend on the economic viability and public acceptability of fast breeder reactors.

There is therefore a need to evaluate other potential sources of electricity, such as tidal power. For these reasons the Severn Barrage Committee was set up in 1978 to advise Government on the desirability of a tidal scheme in the Severn Estuary (Annex 1).

At that time there were major uncertainties about the technical feasibility of constructing a large barrage, the likely costs and benefits and possible impacts on man and the environment. It was therefore considered unwise to embark immediately upon an expensive full-scale feasibility study. Instead a broad 'pre-feasibility' study was indicated with more limited objectives. In essence the aims of this study have been to identify the most promising schemes and study them in sufficient depth to establish whether a full-scale study could be justified (Annex 2).

This pre-feasibility study was started in the autumn of 1978 and has involved a total expenditure of about £2.3M. It has been carried out primarily by means of a large number of contracts with engineering consultants and contractors in industry, universities, government laboratories, the Nature Conservancy Council, institutes of the Natural Environment Research Council etc, and liaison with other relevant organisations such as the Central Electricity Generating Board and the Water Authorities (Annex 3). A feature of this study has been the wide range of subject areas covered and the strong interactions between them.

During this study certain guidelines have been followed:

- A conservative technical approach has been adopted wherever possible. This implies either the use of existing technology or minimal extrapolation from present experience. Hence views on technical feasibility are most firmly based. However, this leaves scope in future for cost reduction in some areas.
- Since the economic viability of tidal power is sensitive to the price of fossil fuels and the proportion of nuclear plant in the generating system, the sensitivity to these and similar assumptions has been examined over a range of scenarios.
- Work on environmental impacts has of necessity been limited to identification and preliminary appraisal of potential problems which might affect the acceptability of particular tidal schemes.

Finally, the reader should note that all the prices and costs quoted in this report are in terms of the value of money in December 1980, except where indicated.

Fig 1 The Preferred Scheme

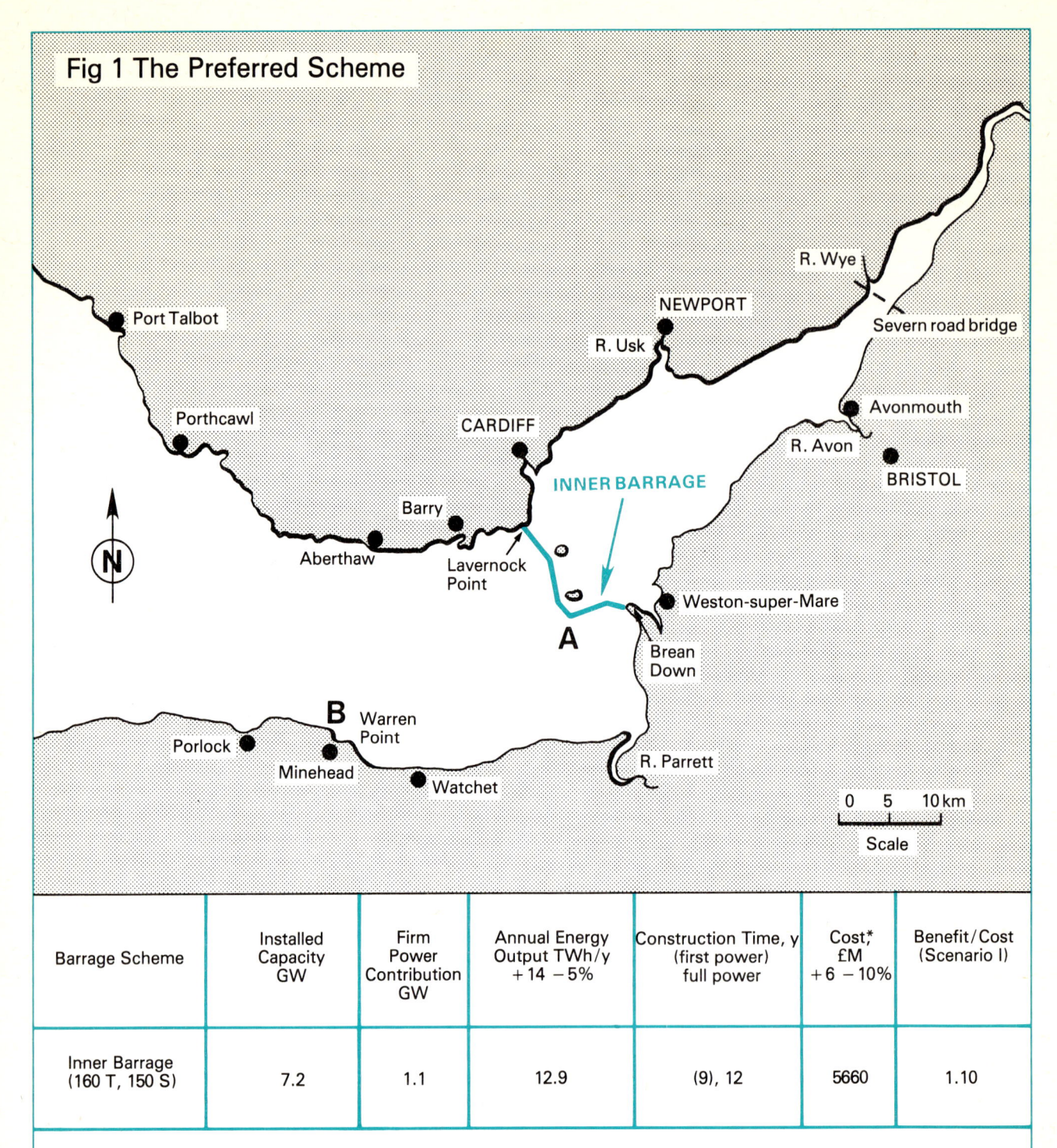

Barrage Scheme	Installed Capacity GW	Firm Power Contribution GW	Annual Energy Output TWh/y +14 −5%	Construction Time, y (first power) full power	Cost* £M +6 −10%	Benefit/Cost (Scenario I)
Inner Barrage (160 T, 150 S)	7.2	1.1	12.9	(9), 12	5660	1.10

T = no. of 9 m 45 MW turbogenerators
S = no. of 12 m square sluice equivalents

Building the Inner Barrage would not preclude the option of obtaining more energy from the estuary by constructing a second stage running from A to B.

*This cost is in terms of December 1980 prices. It includes all direct costs and an allowance of £1,050M for contingencies and post tender costs. However, it does not include either interest during construction or indirect costs, such as those which would result from any additional effluent treatment which might be required.

Summary of Findings 2

Choice of Scheme

1. The Committee concludes that it is technically feasible to enclose the estuary by a barrage located in any position east of a line drawn from Porlock due north to the Welsh Coast. The chief purpose of such a barrage would be the generation of electricity. The barrage would consist of large prefabricated concrete units (caissons) to house the turbines and sluices, together with embankments and ship locks.

2. Comparison of capital costs and energy production show that three schemes are more attractive than any other. These were therefore considered in detail and are:

(a) **Outer Barrage** — a single basin ebb generation scheme based on a barrage running from just east of Minehead to Aberthaw. This would cost about £8,900M*, including an allowance for contingency, and produce about 20 Terawatt hours a year (about 10% of present electricity demand in England and Wales) from an installed capacity of about 12,000 Megawatts. This scheme would effectively exploit the energy potential of the estuary.

(b) **Inner Barrage** — a single basin ebb generation scheme with a barrage running from Brean Down to the vicinity of Lavernock Point on the Welsh Coast. This would cost about £5,600M, including an allowance for contingency, and produce about 13 Terrawatt hours a year (6% of present electricity demand), from an installed capacity of 7,200 Megawatts. This scheme would be the most cost-effective.

(c) **Staged Scheme** — as (b) but with a second basin bounded by a dam branching off from the Inner Barrage near Brean Down and running to just east of Minehead, enclosing Bridgwater Bay. This two-stage scheme would generate almost as much energy as the Outer Barrage and would have a similar economic performance. If this second basin were to be operated in flood generation mode, electricity would be produced in four blocks extending over about 20 hours each day. A decision on this second stage could be deferred for many years without affecting the development of the first stage.

3. The Committee felt that the greater energy output of the Outer Barrage would not compensate for its greater engineering risks, greater environmental impact and lesser economic attractiveness. Accordingly it recommends that attention should be concentrated on the Inner Barrage. The second basin of the Staged Scheme is not attractive on current costings. However, if future circumstances made the second basin desirable, it could be added later so as to exploit the full energy potential of the estuary.

4. A double basin scheme providing an element of energy storage is not of primary interest, since this storage would be two to three times more expensive than other storage options. Even if these other options were not available, storage at this cost is unlikely to be economic.

Economic Viability

5. The major benefit of any of the leading tidal power schemes would be to reduce by 5-8 million tons of coal equivalent per annum the amount of fuel burnt in other power stations within the generating system, thereby saving operating costs. Since nuclear fuel is very much cheaper than coal or oil, the size of the nuclear component of the generating system is decisive for the evaluation of the economics of a Severn Estuary barrage.

6. A tidal barrage operating in the ebb generation mode would produce electricity twice a day for several hours at times largely controlled by the tidal cycle. Therefore, on many occasions the barrage could not contribute to electricity generation at a time of high demand. Thus, construction of a tidal barrage would not reduce the need for future power station capacity by more than about one Gigawatt.

7. The economic prospect for tidal power has improved significantly compared with the view held at the beginning of this study and described in Energy Papers 23 and 27. It is now believed that about 40% more energy might be obtainable from an Inner Barrage than had previously been estimated, for the same capital outlay. Also, the first electricity might be generated within 9 years of the start of construction, rather than 16 years.

8. The unit cost of electricity generated by the most economic tidal power scheme might be around 3.1 pence per kilowatt hour; this is expected to be broadly within the range of future costs of generation (including capital and operating components) from conventional coal and nuclear plant.

*all costs given in this report are in terms of the value of money in December 1980, unless otherwise stated.

Summary of Findings (Continued) 2

9. If the proportion of nuclear plant in the generating system rises only to a limited extent, the Inner Barrage would be an economic investment in the sense that it would meet the Treasury's minimum requirement of a 5% real rate of return and enable total system costs to be reduced. If available, however, the construction of additional nuclear plant would on present estimates be a more economically attractive investment, leading to a larger reduction in total system costs. The view taken about the long term success of the present nuclear strategy is therefore an important judgement which must be made in deciding on the desirability of the barrage.

10. The absolute value of tidal power is sensitive to assumptions about how a number of important parameters will vary in the future:
- the faster *fossil fuel prices* rise, the greater the value of tidal power. The future price of coal is especially significant.
- the faster the *proportion of nuclear plant in the generating system* increases, the lower the value of tidal power.
- a higher *discount rate* of 7% would render tidal power marginally uneconomic, whereas a lower discount rate of 3% would make it an attractive investment.

However, since nuclear power and tidal power are both capital intensive, with the main benefit being a saving in fossil fuels, the values are affected in similar ways by the above changes. Hence the relative value of a tidal to a nuclear investment would be comparatively insensitive to such changes. Nevertheless, in a future with unexpectedly high energy costs the barrage would be of great advantage.

Impacts on Man and the Environment

11. The environmental changes so far predicted either raise questions for which solutions have been identified or are such as not to rule out further consideration of a barrage. However, in the limited timescale of this study a detailed assessment of all the possible effects on man and the environment has not been possible.

12. Although much work remains to be done a number of preliminary judgements are possible:

(a) **Ports and Navigation.** Two large ship locks in the barrage would be needed to give access to ports in the upper estuary. Continued accessibility of these ports would depend critically upon the new tidal levels within the basin which, according to hydraulic modelling experts, can now be predicted to about 0.3m. For the Inner Barrage the slight reductions in maximum water depths would affect larger ships entering these ports if remedial measures are not undertaken. However, average journey times for ships would be no longer than at present, because delays in locking through the barrage would be more than offset by time savings arising from the greater average water depth in the basin.

(b) **Employment.** Building the Inner Barrage would create about 21,000 new jobs, including those in supply industries, for varying periods of up to 10 years. Most of these would be in South Wales. Building the Second Stage immediately afterwards would result in employment for a further decade.

(c) **Resources.** Most of the building materials could be brought to site by sea and their production should not strain resources. An exception could be the provision of rockfill. The manufacture of a large number of turbines at the required rate might also strain UK industrial capacity.

(d) **Recreation.** The lower tidal range and reduced current would make the estuary much more attractive for water based recreation and would also provide opportunity for additional employment.

(e) **Water Quality in the Estuary.** At present pollutants discharged into the estuary are rapidly dispersed by strong tidal currents and this dispersion would be reduced by a barrage. On the other hand, dilution of effluent would be greater with a barrage due to higher average water levels. Maintenance of the quality of tidal waters in their present general state would not be technically difficult and could be achieved by introducing more treatment of sewage and industrial waste, at a cost of £120-230M for plant with running costs of £12-24M per year. However, the need to maintain any specific aspect of tidal water quality in its present state would be a question of choice, demanding a policy decision. Reductions in salinity and turbidity would be inevitable.

Summary of Findings (Continued) **2**

(f) **Land Drainage.** Extra pumping would be required to clear surface water runoff from some areas behind the Inner Barrage. This would require an investment of around £14-19M. The Second Stage would improve land drainage in the Somerset Levels, although this could be to the detriment of nature conservation interests.

(g) **Sea Defence.** A barrage would reduce the risk of salt water flooding low lying land behind the barrage during extreme tides. However, long lengths of sea-defence banks in the estuary are protected by vegetation. Some of these might have to be provided with more permanent protection against longer periods of wave attack at high water, at a cost that might reach £10M.

(h) **Sediments.** The gentler tidal regime would result in greatly reduced rates of sediment transport. With a barrage much of the silt and mud presently moving about the estuary in large quantities during each tide would settle. The amounts of new sediments entering the estuary are relatively small. Local effects, for example in port approach channels, have not yet been investigated to determine the need, if any, for remedial measures.

(j) **Birds.** The reduction in areas of intertidal banks, together with reduced salinity in the basin, might lead to a decrease in the numbers of wading birds and shelduck. However, substantial increases in the population of both bottom-feeding and especially suspension-feeding organisms are forecast. This could have the effect of increasing both the variety of species present in the estuary and the total bird population. Expert opinion is divided on the extent of any change.

(k) **Migratory Fish.** Migrating salmon should be able to pass upstream through the large sluices in the barrage. Young salmon (smolts) heading to sea might resist the downward flow of water and thus avoid the turbines. Fish passes might deal with the problem. Another potential difficulty, yet to be evaluated, is whether salmon could become trapped in any Second Stage basin.

13. The social and industrial impacts of a barrage, including the effects on employment, on the future development of industry around the estuary, on land resources, on local communities (especially during construction) and on existing amenities, would all need careful consideration.

14. From this enumeration of the effects of a barrage it is clear that its environmental, social and industrial acceptability has not yet been established. This must therefore be a major objective of any future work.

Recommendations

15. On the grounds that:
   (a) the technical feasibility of a barrage is not in doubt,
   (b) a barrage could provide some insurance against a future in which electricity prices are unexpectedly high,
   (c) a barrage would add to the diversity of types of electricity generation plant, and thus reduce the risk of system failure,
   (d) in many scenarios the Inner Barrage is likely to be an economic investment, although not as good an investment as nuclear plant,
   (e) the Inner Barrage is the most attractive scheme because it would have the least engineering risk and the least adverse impact on man and the environment, and would be the most cost effective,

the Committee unanimously recommends that a further phase of work should be undertaken forthwith and that this should be concentrated on the Inner Barrage.

16. Since the Committee is greatly concerned by the as yet imperfectly understood impacts of a barrage, it feels strongly that it must recommend early setting in train of deeper studies to establish the acceptability of the Inner Barrage. These would include investigation of environmental, social and industrial factors coupled with preliminary design and further economic evaluation. The aim would be to put Government as soon as possible in a position where it could responsibly decide whether to authorise the building of a barrage.

17. Such a combined *Acceptability and Preliminary Design Study* should not take more than four years or cost more than £20M. Half way through this study a decision would be needed on whether to proceed with handling and foundation trials of a prototype caisson in the estuary at a further cost of £25M; bringing these trials forward in this way would substantially shorten the overall time to first generation.

Fig 2 Tidal Resonance in the Severn Estuary

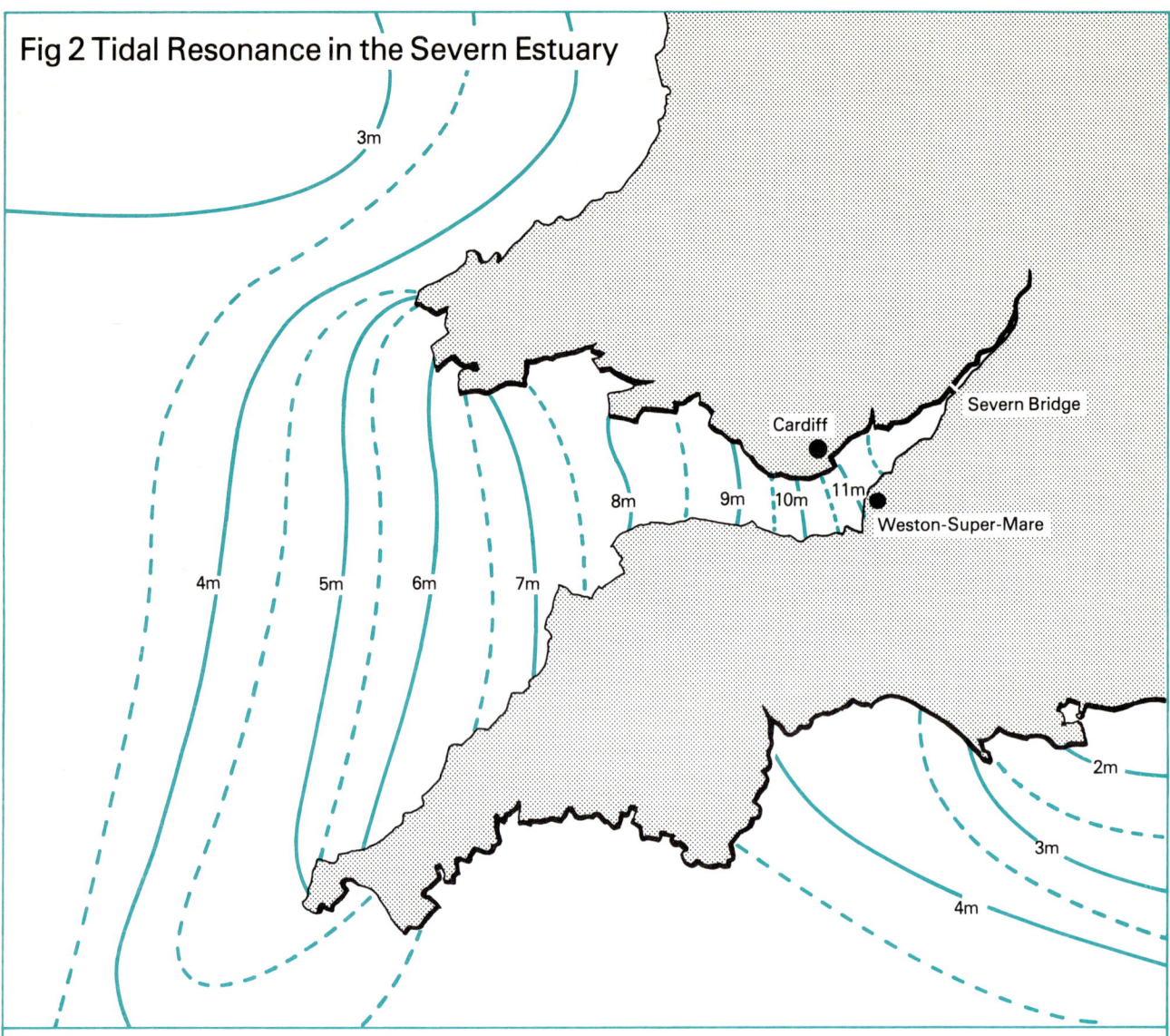

Mean Spring tidal range shown at intervals of 0.5 m

The Tidal Resonance Effect

Part of the reason for the high tidal range in the Severn is that the estuary is close to resonance, resulting in amplification of the tide. In the simple case of a channel of uniform cross-section, resonance occurs if its length is close to one quarter of the wavelength of the tidal movement. A real estuary is more complex and this exact length is modified by the actual variations in width and depth. The rise and fall of the tide is limited by the damping effect caused by frictional losses arising from water moving over the sea-bed.

The extent to which the tidal range is magnified depends on the balance between energy losses and the concentration of the tidal energy. A point of maximum range often occurs beyond which energy is dissipated more quickly than topography concentrates it. In estuaries this point tends to be near where the funnel-like form of the main body gives way to the more parallel-sided flat-bottomed river section. In the Severn, the maximum range occurs in the vicinity of the Severn Bridge.

Impact of a Barrage

In an estuary which is close to resonance, any change in its effective length is likely to move the estuary nearer to or further from resonance with the tides, so increasing or decreasing the tidal range. This suggests that building a barrage might have a significant effect on the tidal range and implies that the magnitude of this effect will depend on the location of the barrage.

Any modification to the tidal range and water movement pattern in the estuary would affect many important aspects including not only the energy output but also navigation, land drainage, disposal of pollutants, sediment patterns and movement and a variety of environmental factors. These impacts would be most marked inside the barrage.

Tidal Modelling

Predictions have been carried out using computerised numerical models to simulate the behaviour of the tides in the estuary and the sea approaches. The models represent the water movement in two dimensions but not any variation of velocity with depth.

Tides in the Severn Estuary 3

The Tidal Cycles

18. Tides arise because the Earth's rotation moves its surface through a complex gravitational field determined by the relative positions of the Earth, the Moon and the Sun. The relative motions of these bodies give rise to various tidal cycles. These are:—

(a) **A Semi-Diurnal Cycle,** due primarily to the rotation of the Earth within the gravitational field of the Moon, which produces a high water to high water period of about 12 hours 25 minutes.

(b) **A Spring-Neap Cycle,** due to the occurrence of maxima and minima in the combined effect of the gravitational fields of the Moon and the Sun, which give rise to a period of about 14 days between successive spring tides. This is modified on a monthly basis because the Moon's orbit is an ellipse. Thus successive spring-neap cycles can vary in amplitude by around $\pm 15\%$.

(c) **A Semi-Annual Cycle,** due to the inclination of the Moon's orbit to that of the Earth, which gives rise to a period of about 178 days between the highest spring tides, which occur in March and September.

(d) **Other Cycles,** such as the *19 year* and *1600 year* cycles, which arise from further complex interactions between the gravitational fields.

In general the range of a spring tide is about twice that of a neap tide, whereas the longer period cycles impose smaller perturbations, such as $\pm 11\%$ due to the semi-annual cycle and $\pm 4\%$ due to the 19 year cycle.

Tides in the Severn Estuary

19. The amplitudes of these cycles are increased substantially, particularly in estuaries, by local effects such as shelving, funnelling, reflection and resonance. The combined effect of these factors in the Severn Estuary gives rise to one of the largest tidal ranges in the world. The map in Fig 2 shows that the 4m tidal range at the mouth of the Bristol Channel is amplified to over 11m in the vicinity of the Severn Bridge.

The Extractable Energy

20. The amount of energy available from the tides is approximately proportional to the square of the tidal range. The energy available for extraction by a tidal power plant would vary by a factor of around four over the spring-neap cycle. Moreover, since the time of high water advances about an hour each day, it would not in general be possible to tailor the energy output of a tidal plant to the daily pattern of power demand. Unlike most other renewable energy sources, however, tides are predictable and therefore the total electricity generating system could be pre-scheduled to make optimum use of tidal energy.

Effect of a Barrage

21. Numerical modelling studies have shown that the tidal range would be reduced by a barrage and that this reduction would become more pronounced the further seaward the barrage is located. Typically, an ebb generation barrage in the region of Cardiff to Weston-super-Mare would reduce the mean tidal range outside the barrage by about 11%, whereas a similar barrage from Minehead to Aberthaw wouid produce a 20% reduction. These reductions are important because of the significant diminution in energy output which would result.

Fig 3 Other Modes of Operation of a Simple Barrage

Flood Generation

Flood generation, by restricting the tidal levels to below present mean sea level, would have a very severe impact on all ports above the barrage and lead to major visual and ecological impacts. If these adverse effects were counterbalanced by a greater energy output than is available from alternative modes of operation, one might still consider flood generation further. However, a flood generation scheme would provide less energy than the equivalent ebb generation scheme. This is because the surface area of the estuary decreases with depth and this has two substantial effects:—
(i) the water level would rise fastest in the early stages of flood generation whereas in ebb generation the reverse is true,
(ii) the volume of water to pass through the turbines would be less in a flood scheme than it is in an equivalent ebb-generation scheme.

The lower energy potential of flood generation schemes, plus the severe navigational and environmental impacts, mean that this mode of operation can be discounted for a simple barrage across the estuary.

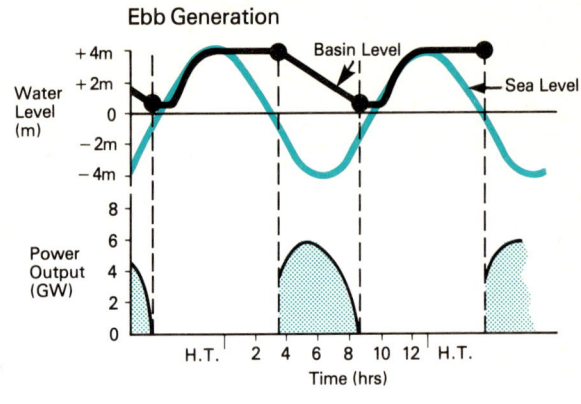

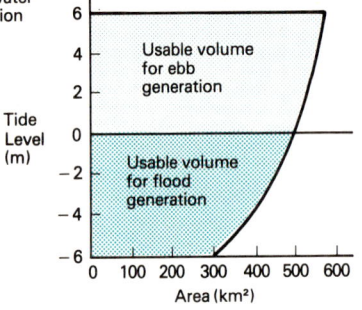

Two-Way Generation

The main attraction of two-way generation is that it would enable electricity to be produced during a greater proportion of the day and permit greater operational flexibility.

However, there are a number of disadvantages:
(i) Modelling studies have shown that, for a barrage containing any given number of turbines, slightly *less* energy would be produced by two-way generation than by simple ebb generation. This is because the head of water at the start of generation in either direction is much less with two-way generation than with simple ebb or flood generation. This is caused by the need to maintain a useful head of water in the reverse direction during the preceding period of generation. Also, with two-way generation the turbines would operate less efficiently at any given head, because the turbine blades and water passageways can only be fully optimised for a single direction of flow.
(ii) Two-way generation has been shown to be typically 15-20% more expensive for a barrage of given energy output, mostly as a result of the larger number of turbines and turbine caissons of higher unit cost which would be required. These increases in cost would not be fully offset by savings in the cost of sluices and electrical transmission.
(iii) The impact on ports and navigation would be severe, with the highest tides behind the barrage restricted to about mid-way between the present mid and high tides.

On balance the higher unit cost of energy production and damage to ports are considered to outweigh any advantages of operational flexibility.

Pumping

Pumping may be associated with any of the above schemes. However, it can be shown that for the favoured ebb generation method of operation there would be little or no energy gain. This is because, if the turbines are to be optimised for maximum energy output, their pumping efficiencies will be very low. Should the pumping efficiencies be improved this would lead to a lower generating efficiency and loss on overall energy output. This, considered together with the requirement for a more complex and expensive machine and the fact that the timing of the tides rarely make the pumping mode of operation convenient for the rest of the system, means that pumping is not considered an economic option. However, it may still be desirable to restore high water levels at neap tides to their present values in order to maintain access for large ships to the ports.

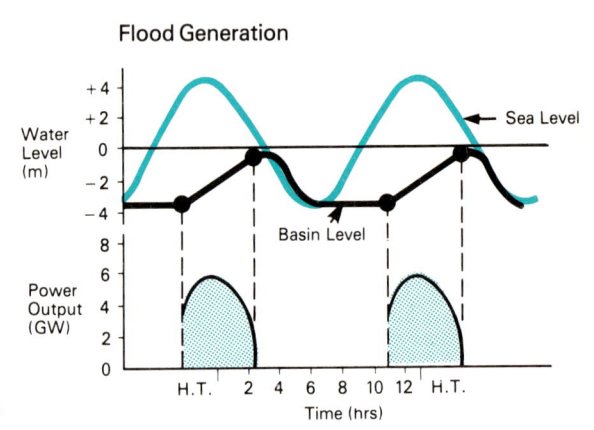

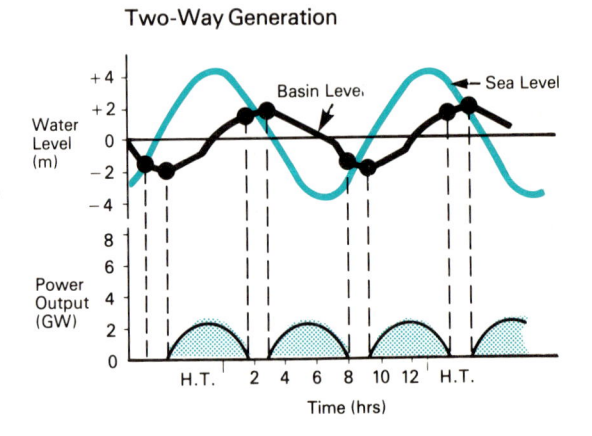

Water Levels and Energy Outputs for Different Modes of Barrage Operation

Energy Extraction 4

22. Single basin tidal power schemes may be designed to operate in one of three different modes:—

Ebb generation. This mode of operation allows the rising tide to flow in through sluices and turbines, which idle in reverse. Both sluices and turbine passageways are then closed soon after high tide. These are kept closed until the tide has ebbed sufficiently for the difference in water level between the barrage and the sea to drive the turbines and their generators. The water is then allowed to flow through the turbines until the difference in water level is too low to turn them efficiently, when they are closed down. This will be when the water in the basin is at about the present mid-tide level.

Flood generation operates in the reverse mode. Water is allowed out of the basin through the sluices until low tide. The sluices are then closed against the incoming tide so that the water level outside the barrage rises above that in the basin. When the appropriate head of water for driving the turbines has been achieved, they commence operation and continue until the water level in the basin has reached about mid-tide. At this time the head of water across the barrage is no longer adequate to drive the turbines.

Two-way generation combines both modes of operation by generating over parts of both the rising and falling tide. Toward the end of a period of ebb generation the sluices will be opened in order to reduce the basin level quickly to prepare for the period of flood generation. This curtails the period over which ebb generation might otherwise have occurred. A similar situation occurs at the end of flood generation when it is necessary to open the sluices to fill the basin as quickly as possible prior to the ebb operation.

23. In each case the turbines could be designed to pump water in the opposite direction to the flow during generation. If pumping takes place when the basin and sea levels are nearly the same, and if the water is used later in the tidal cycle when the head is greater, then an energy gain is in theory possible. Also pumping would enable part of the energy output to be retimed by an hour or two. However, in practice pumping is unlikely to be cost effective.

24. Of the three methods of operation, *ebb generation* without pumping is preferred for the following reasons:

- it gives the minimum unit cost for energy generation
- it has least impact on navigation (tides in the basin range from near present mid-tide to present high tide)
- it has least detrimental visual impact.

25. The box opposite summarises why flood and two-way generation are less favourable than ebb generation and also why pumping would not be economic.

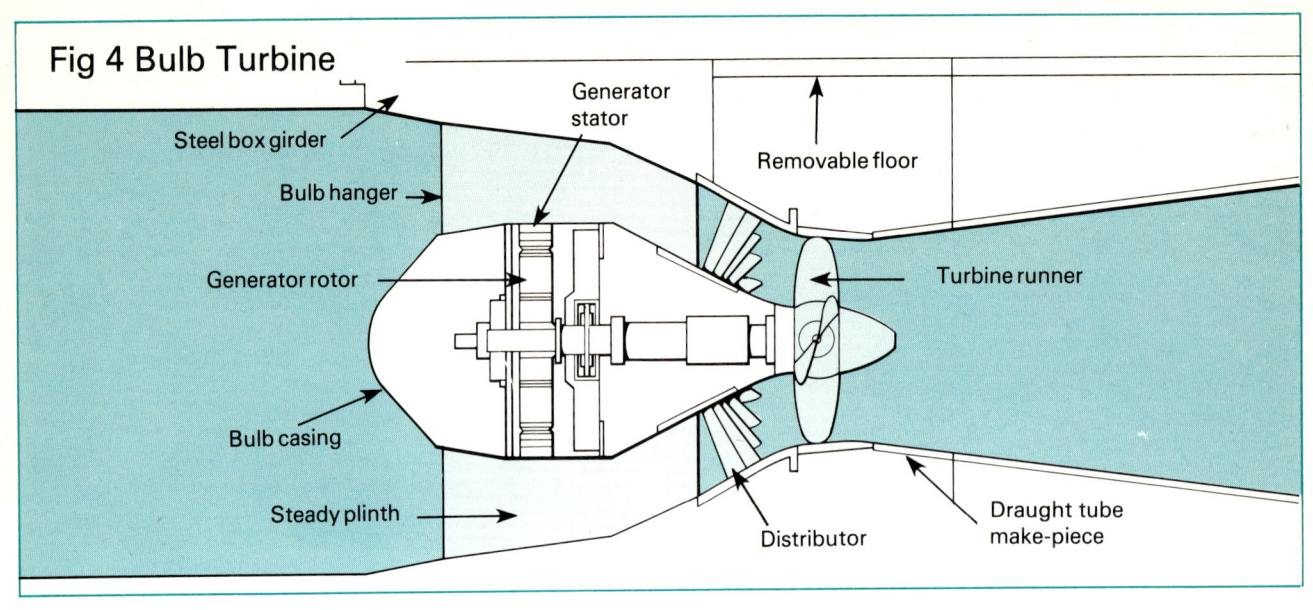

Fig 4 Bulb Turbine

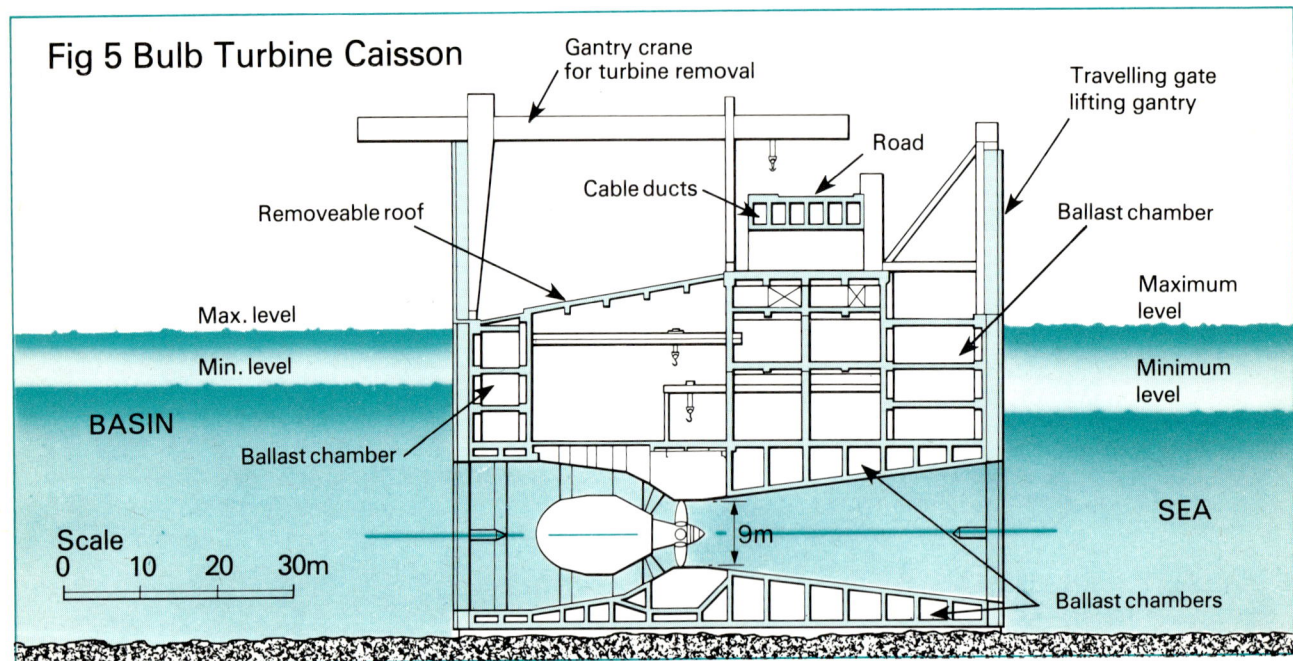

- Steel box girder
- Bulb hanger
- Generator stator
- Generator rotor
- Bulb casing
- Steady plinth
- Removable floor
- Turbine runner
- Distributor
- Draught tube make-piece

Fig 5 Bulb Turbine Caisson

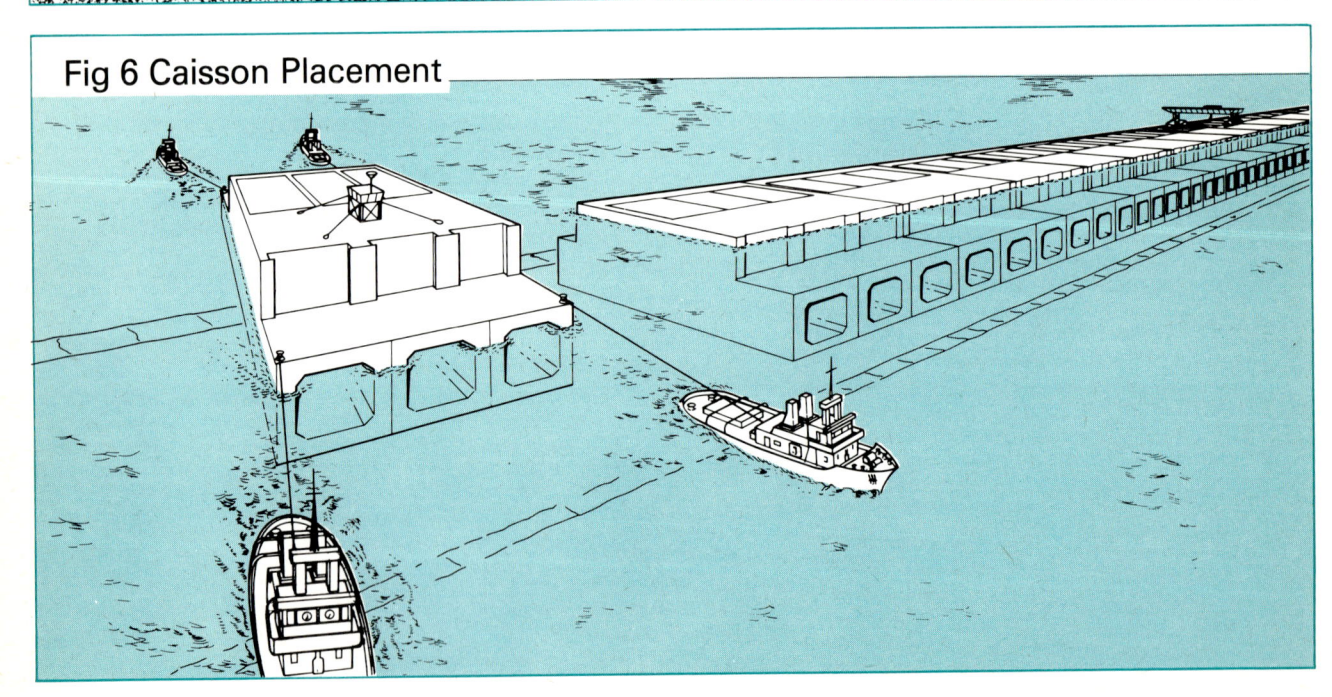

- Gantry crane for turbine removal
- Removeable roof
- Cable ducts
- Road
- Travelling gate lifting gantry
- Ballast chamber
- Max. level
- Min. level
- BASIN
- Ballast chamber
- Maximum level
- Minimum level
- SEA
- 9m
- Ballast chambers

Scale 0 10 20 30m

Fig 6 Caisson Placement

10

Components and Construction of a Barrage (Continued)

26. Tidal energy is primarily of interest as a source for generating electricity. This energy is most efficiently and economically extracted by the construction of a barrage to create a hydrostatic head of water which can be used to operate turbines to generate electricity.

Components of a Barrage

27. Necessary major components of such a barrage include:
    - *sluices* which let water into or out of the enclosed basin as required.
    - *turbo-generators* comprising turbines which convert the flow of water into shaft rotation and generators which convert this rotation into electricity. These need to be located in the deepest water to avoid cavitation.
    - *ship-locks* to permit continued navigation to existing ports within the basin.
    - *embankments* to complete the barrage across the estuary and provide access to the turbines, sluices and ship locks.

28. The barrage itself would be constructed from a combination of *caissons*, which are large preformed concrete structures which can be floated into position, and *embankments*. The caissons would house the turbo-generators and associated electrical installations, such as transformers and switchgear, and the sluices.

29. Once the approximate barrage line has been selected on the basis of considerations of energy output, costs and environmental impacts, the exact line then needs to be selected to take account of the contours and geology of the estuary bed, the number and requirements of the above components and local environmental factors.

Turbo-generators

30. Three different types of turbo-generator, namely bulb, rim-generator and tubular, have been considered.* The barrage designs and costs for this study have been based on the bulb type, (Fig 4) which has been proven with large units in both low-head run-of-river applications and the tidal scheme at La Rance. The largest units made so far are 7.7m in diameter. For the Severn Barrage a turbine diameter of 9.0m would be a reasonable extrapolation of existing technology, subject to satisfactory prototype testing. This larger turbine should be more economic than one of around 7.5m, although the overall effect on the economics of tidal power would be small.

31. There is some evidence that the use of rim-generator ("Straflo") turbines could lead to significant cost reductions for both the turbo-generators and their associated caissons. This possibility requires further study. All existing installations operate at fixed speed, synchronised with the grid. This study has shown that variable speed operation, with d.c. transmission links, has some advantages and could well be a feasible alternative for a tidal barrage.

32. The large number of identical machines would give scope to reduce unit costs by production line techniques. Further savings should result if the turbines could be designed for transport by sea, either in large pieces or as complete units, rather than for road transport.

---

*see glossary, Annex 9

Fig 7 Types of Sluice Caisson

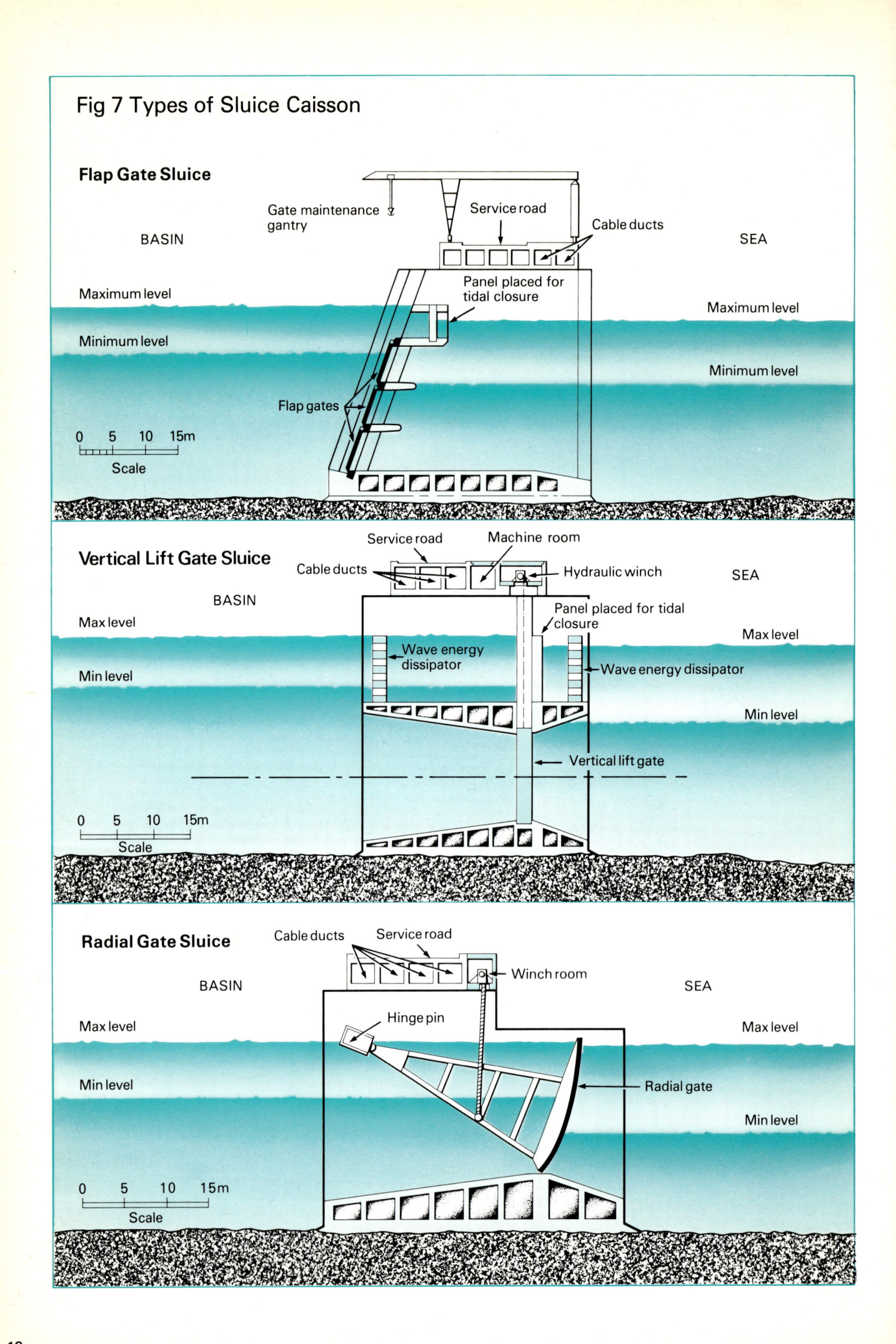

Components and Construction of a Barrage (Continued)

Turbine Caissons

33. The concept of building concrete caissons in land-based work yards and towing them into position dates back to the wartime Mulberry Harbour and in recent times the Dutch have gained considerable experience in this area. This concept is central to the construction of a barrage in the Severn Estuary. These caissons would be massive structures. When complete and ready for towing a caisson for three turbines would weigh about 90,000 tonnes and draw around 22m of water (Figs 5 & 6). However, since this is only about one-third the size of concrete oil production platforms used in the North Sea, the manufacture of these caissons is well within the capability of the UK construction industry.

34. Caissons would be required to house two or three turbines each, the larger version showing a slight benefit in overall cost, construction time and stability during towing.

Sluice Caissons

35. Sluices would also be built quickly and economically as caissons. A wide variety of gate types could be used, of which three are most appropriate to a tidal scheme, namely flap, vertical lift and radial gates (Fig 7, see also Glossary Annex 9). The barrage costing has been based on the vertical lift gate, but it is possible that all three types would be used depending on location and water depth.

Ship Locks

36. Two ship locks, each about 366m × 50m, would be required to maintain access for the predicted levels of shipping to ports enclosed by the barrage. Various construction techniques could be used but in this study a design similar to that used for the recent Royal Portbury Dock at Bristol has been assumed, built in a sand island protected by suitable armouring and breakwaters.

Embankments

37. A relatively conservative embankment design (Fig 8) has been used as a basis for estimating costs, partly because these represent only about 15% of total costs and partly because any unforeseen delay in achieving closure would be costly. However, alternative designs have been suggested which might achieve useful economies and deserve further study.

38. The main building materials for the embankments would be rock for the initial mound needed to achieve control over the tidal flows and make the final 'closure' of the estuary, together with sand-fill for the main body of the embankment.

39. Sources of the large quantities of rock required have not yet been positively identified. There could be problems in obtaining supplies locally, as existing quarries are not geared to producing the large sizes of rock rubble required, and because of environmental considerations. More distant sources, possibly including foreign ones, could be used because transport by sea from coastal quarries direct to the site could be cheaper than multiple handling from inland sources.

40. Sand should be available from dredging within the estuary. An alternative might be to use easily available waste materials from local mining or china clay industries, but the cost of transport would make these more expensive.

41. Alternatively, simple blank caissons could be used instead of embankment in water deeper than about 15m to reduce costs.

Fig 8 Main Embankment Cross Section

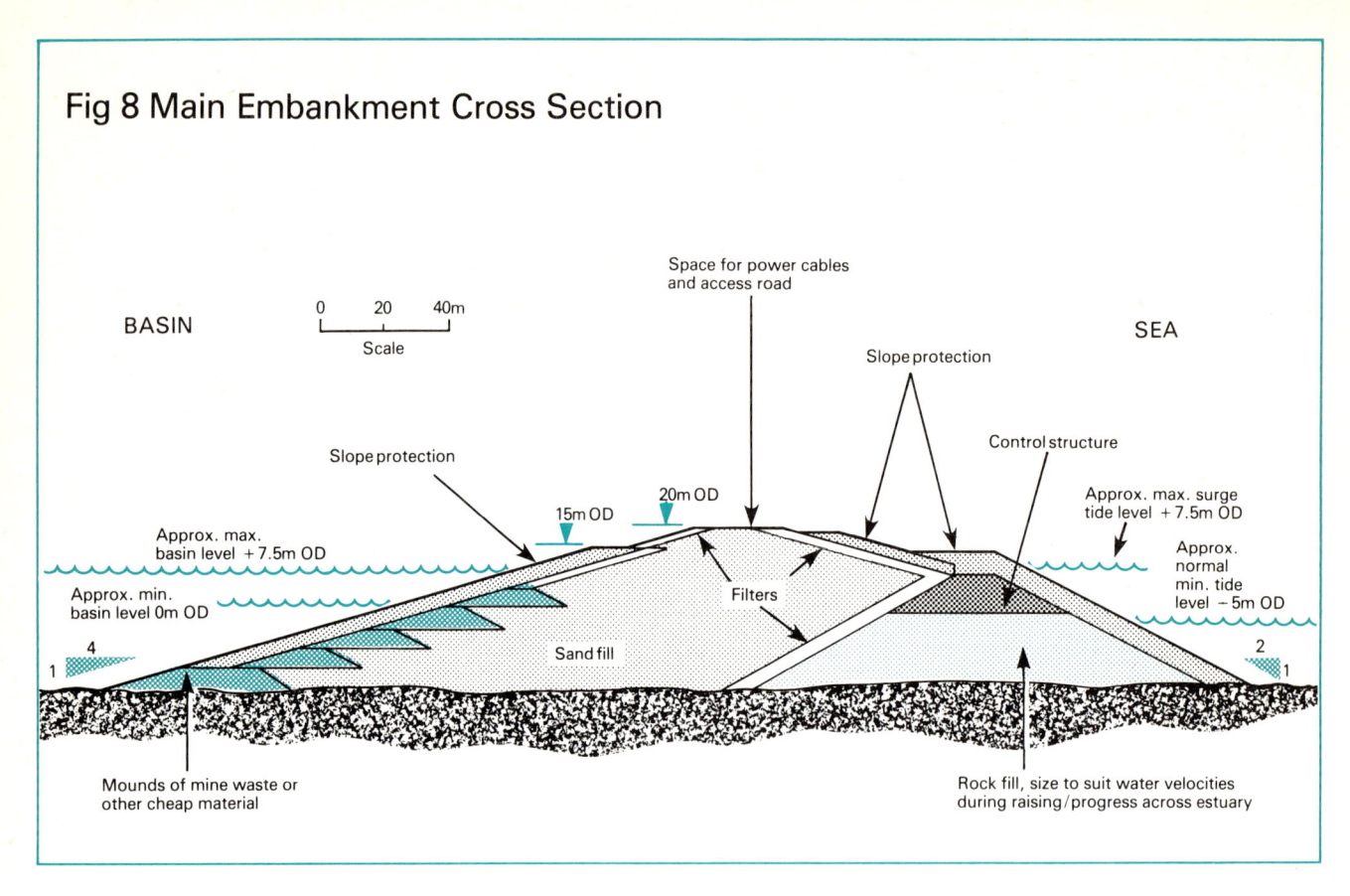

BASIN

Scale 0 20 40m

SEA

Space for power cables and access road

Slope protection

Slope protection

Control structure

Approx. max. basin level +7.5m OD

15m OD

20m OD

Approx. max. surge tide level +7.5m OD

Approx. min. basin level 0m OD

Filters

Approx. normal min. tide level −5m OD

Sand fill

4
1

2
1

Mounds of mine waste or other cheap material

Rock fill, size to suit water velocities during raising/progress across estuary

Fig 9 Construction Programme for the Inner Barrage

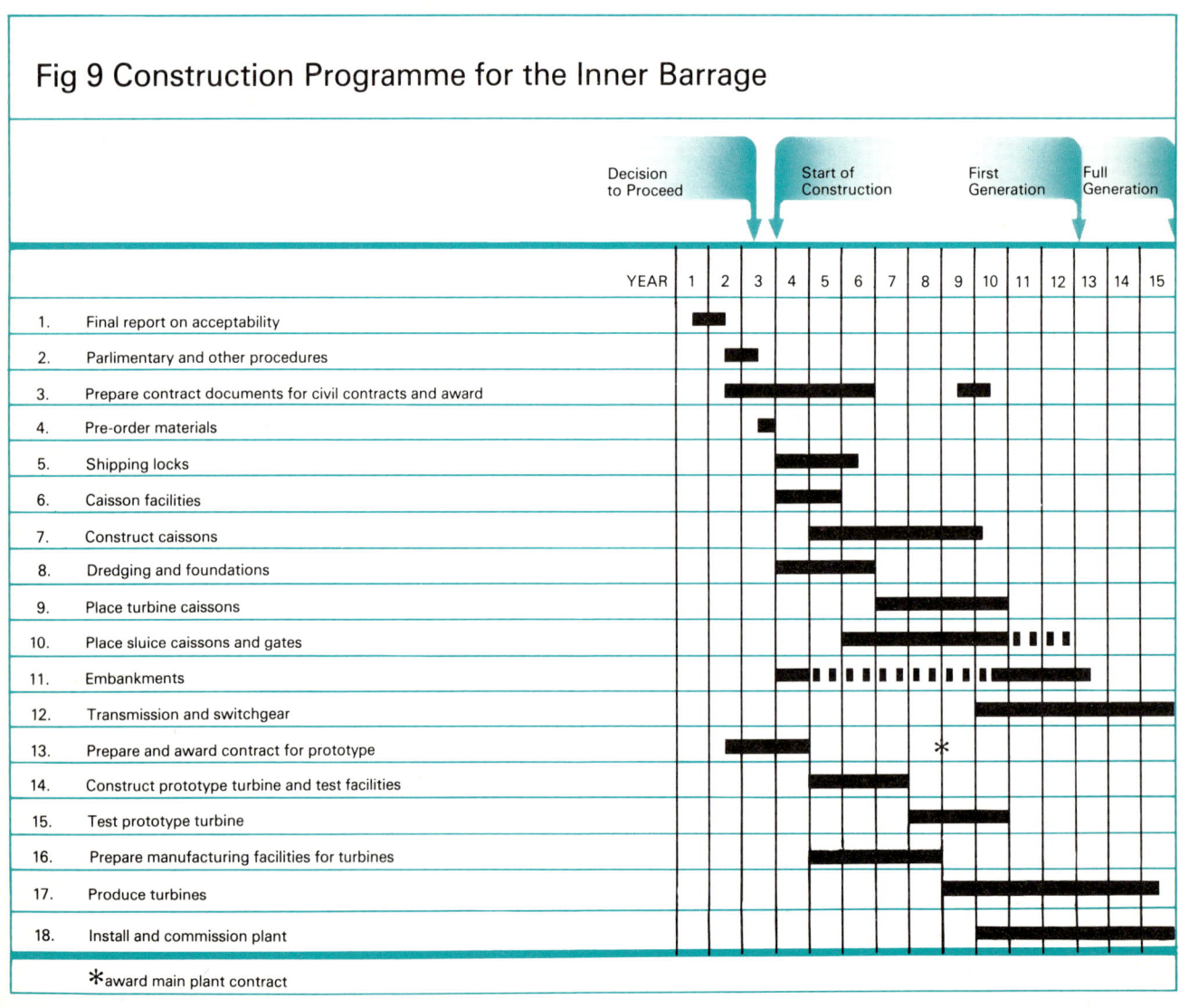

		YEAR	1	2	3	4	5	6	7	8	9	10	11	12	13	14	15
1.	Final report on acceptability																
2.	Parliamentary and other procedures																
3.	Prepare contract documents for civil contracts and award																
4.	Pre-order materials																
5.	Shipping locks																
6.	Caisson facilities																
7.	Construct caissons																
8.	Dredging and foundations																
9.	Place turbine caissons																
10.	Place sluice caissons and gates																
11.	Embankments																
12.	Transmission and switchgear																
13.	Prepare and award contract for prototype										*						
14.	Construct prototype turbine and test facilities																
15.	Test prototype turbine																
16.	Prepare manufacturing facilities for turbines																
17.	Produce turbines																
18.	Install and commission plant																

Decision to Proceed — Start of Construction — First Generation — Full Generation

*award main plant contract

Components and Construction of a Barrage   5

Transmission

42. The transmission of the power ashore from a barrage would be by cables laid either in reinforced concrete ducts over the caissons or in the ground along the embankment crest. The cables would change to overhead lines at suitably located substations inshore. With the use of the latest technology such substations could be made much more compact than existing ones. Some strengthening of the 400 kV supergrid would be necessary in Wales and the south-west of England. Alternatively, if a d.c. transmission link were to be used, no new substations would be needed adjacent to the barrage. Instead, the necessary invertors would be located at junctions with the supergrid.

Construction Period

43. Estimates of the resources and time required to construct the Inner Barrage (Brean Down to the vicinity of Lavernock Point) indicate that the programme shown in Fig 9 is feasible. A two year period is needed for initial mobilisation, building work yards and obtaining special equipment. First electricity could be generated by about half the turbines nine years after the decision to proceed, with full power being generated three years later.

Prototype Trials

44. Two elements of a barrage have been identified as meriting prototype trials, because satisfactory performance cannot adequately be proven by appropriate design studies, computer simulations or model tests, namely: —

    (a) the placing of large caissons in the severe tidal conditions of the Severn Estuary, combined with the preparation and subsequent sealing of foundations underneath

    (b) turbo-generator trials, unless a design and size is chosen which has been well proven in run-of-river schemes (e.g. fixed speed 7.5m diameter bulb turbines).

45. The cost of building, handling and placing a simplified prototype turbine caisson is estimated at about £25M. For the turbo-generator trials to be fully valid they should be carried out in the Severn Estuary. This is only practical if another caisson equipped with pumps is built and connected to the turbine caisson so that the turbine can be tested at any desired head and flow at almost any time. The cost of this, including 3 years operation, is estimated at £130M.

46. Prototype trials for turbo-generator plant of a type and size which are proven on overseas run-of-river installations, though not in Severn Estuary conditions, are considered to be cost effective because such trials reduce uncertainty and hence enable allowances for risks and for the cost of post-tender design changes to be reduced. Also, such trials would be essential if plant of an unproven type or size were to be chosen. The cost of prototype trials of a turbine could be a stumbling block to progress if such trials had to be undertaken before the taking of a decision to proceed with the building of a barrage. Studies show that there is reasonable opportunity to design and build a prototype turbine and test it for up to a year between the decision to proceed with a barrage and the time that the assembly of production turbines starts. The commitment of expenditure for establishing turbine manufacturing facilities before the placing of the main plant contract would be reduced if tenders for the prototype and production turbines could be called for before the decision to proceed with a barrage.

Fig 10 Sequence of Construction

The difficulties of the main operations of caisson placing and embankment construction vary significantly as the blockage of the estuary increases. The order in which these activities may be carried out is largely determined by the tidal hydraulics. For example, placement of the large turbine caissons late in the construction sequence would be difficult because of the faster tidal flows.

The main features of the construction sequences are:—

1. Construction of the ship locks on a sand island protected by armouring. This would be done first to ensure minimum disruption to navigation while the barrage is being built.

2. Placement of turbine caissons, without turbines and with draft tubes open to tidal flow. Turbines would be installed as they became available.

3. Placement of sluice caissons, the actual sluice-way then remaining open, with a large upper waterway forming a temporary opening.

4. Construction of the lower parts of the embankment dams in the remaining sections of the barrage, by barge dumping of rock fill.

5. Construction of the upper parts of the embankments by end-dumping of rock to above high water level, probably using land-based plant, and with the waterways through the caissons acting as a tidal by-pass.

6. Completion of the barrage by installing sluice gates, closing temporary openings and finishing the embankments.

About half the turbines might be installed and operational by the time the estuary is closed, giving some power generation. Full output should be attained three years later.

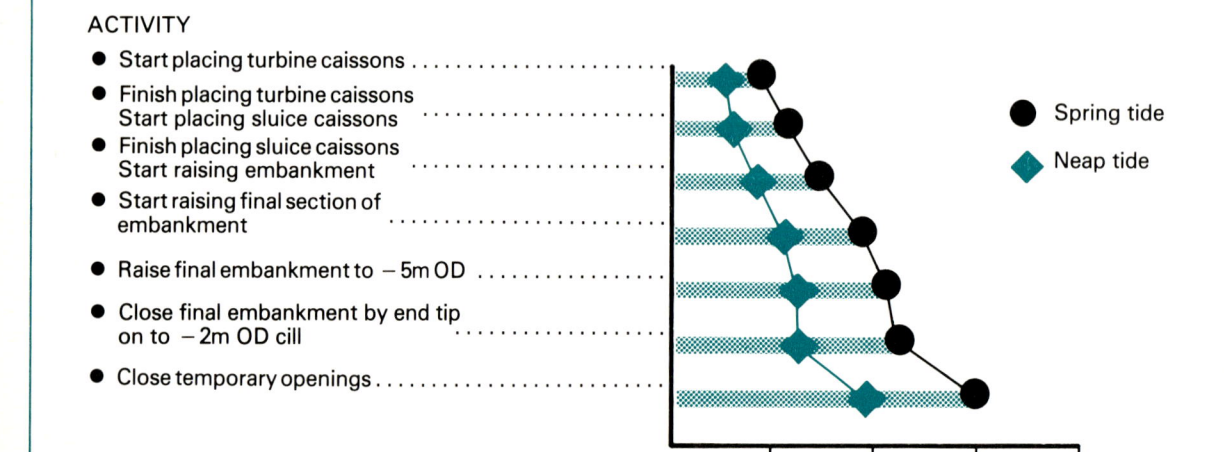

Fig 11 Water Velocities During Construction

ACTIVITY
- Start placing turbine caissons
- Finish placing turbine caissons / Start placing sluice caissons
- Finish placing sluice caissons / Start raising embankment
- Start raising final section of embankment
- Raise final embankment to −5m OD
- Close final embankment by end tip on to −2m OD cill
- Close temporary openings

Spring tide
Neap tide

Max velocity m/s (Inner Barrage)

Technical Feasibility of Estuary Closure 6

47. During construction of a barrage across the estuary the remaining gap available to the tidal flow would be reduced. Thus as construction proceeds the velocities through the gap would increase. The chosen sequence of construction must ensure that each component of the barrage would be built and installed without undue risk or difficulty.

Construction Sequence

48. The main criteria for designing the construction sequence, illustrated opposite, are:—
    (a) minimum disruption of navigation
    (b) adoption of low risk procedures for the last critical stages of 'closure'
    (c) earliest possible closure and hence earliest start of electricity generation.

49. The requirements of low risk and early closure conflict to some extent. In this study, feasibility has been assessed on the basis of a low risk approach. The general philosophy has therefore been to keep as much gap open to flow as possible during each stage of construction. This minimises water velocities and hence reduces the risk and difficulty of each operation.

Technical Feasibility

50. The proven technology of today, including that learnt from the Delta scheme in the Netherlands and from UK operations in the North Sea, is such that it can be stated with confidence that construction of a barrage would be feasible using the building methods and closure sequence just described. Feasibility has been established not only for a barrage in the Cardiff to Weston area but also for barrages much further westward.

51. Closure of the estuary and start of electricity generation should be possible in 9 years for a Cardiff to Weston barrage using this conservative, low risk approach. More rapid closure, e.g. by concurrent construction of caisson and embankment sections, might also be possible at increased risk. This would give earlier power generation and thus improve the economic viability of the scheme. Further work would be required to determine whether the increased risk of the concurrent construction approach could be justified.

52. The feasibility of closure relies on the presence of open waterways in barrage elements already placed (sluices and turbine passageways). Closure of schemes which do not have sluices (e.g. some types of double basin storage schemes) might not, therefore, be possible. Feasibility is, however, firmly established for ebb generation and flood generation barrages.

Fig 12 Notional Barrage Lines and Areas of Most Interest

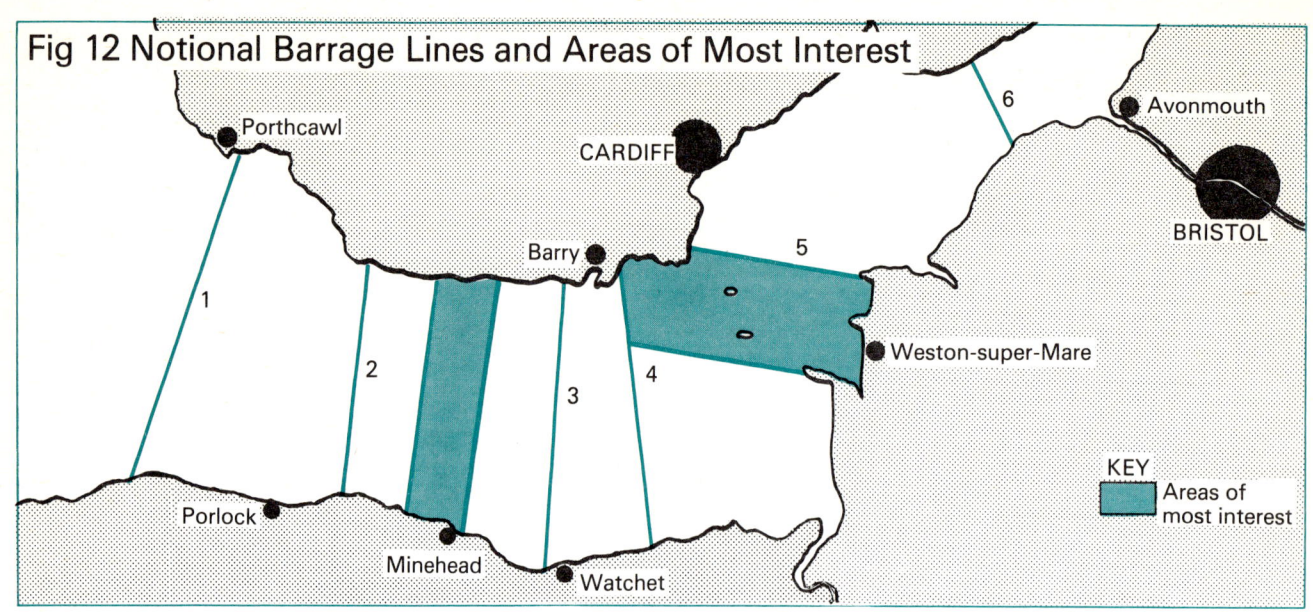

KEY: Areas of most interest

Fig 13 Energy Output and Economic Performance of Notional Barrage Lines

KEY
— energy output, TWh/year
--- barrage cost, £Billion
▨ unit cost of generation, p/kWh

Note: data shown for barrages with maximum practical number of turbines

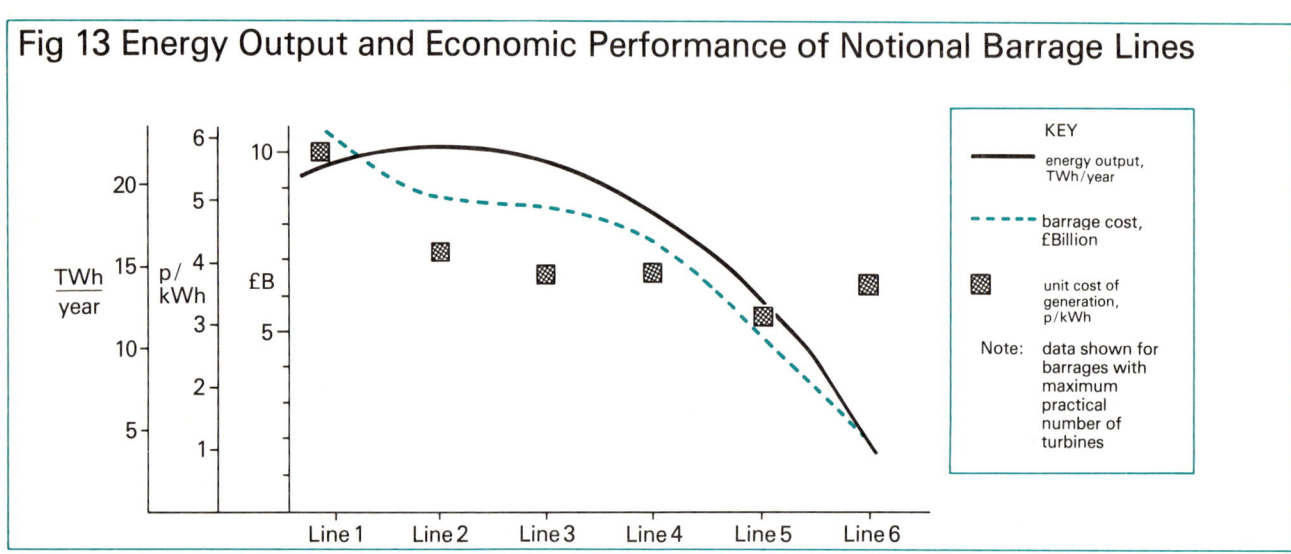

Fig 14 Energy Output and Economic Performance of Different Barrages

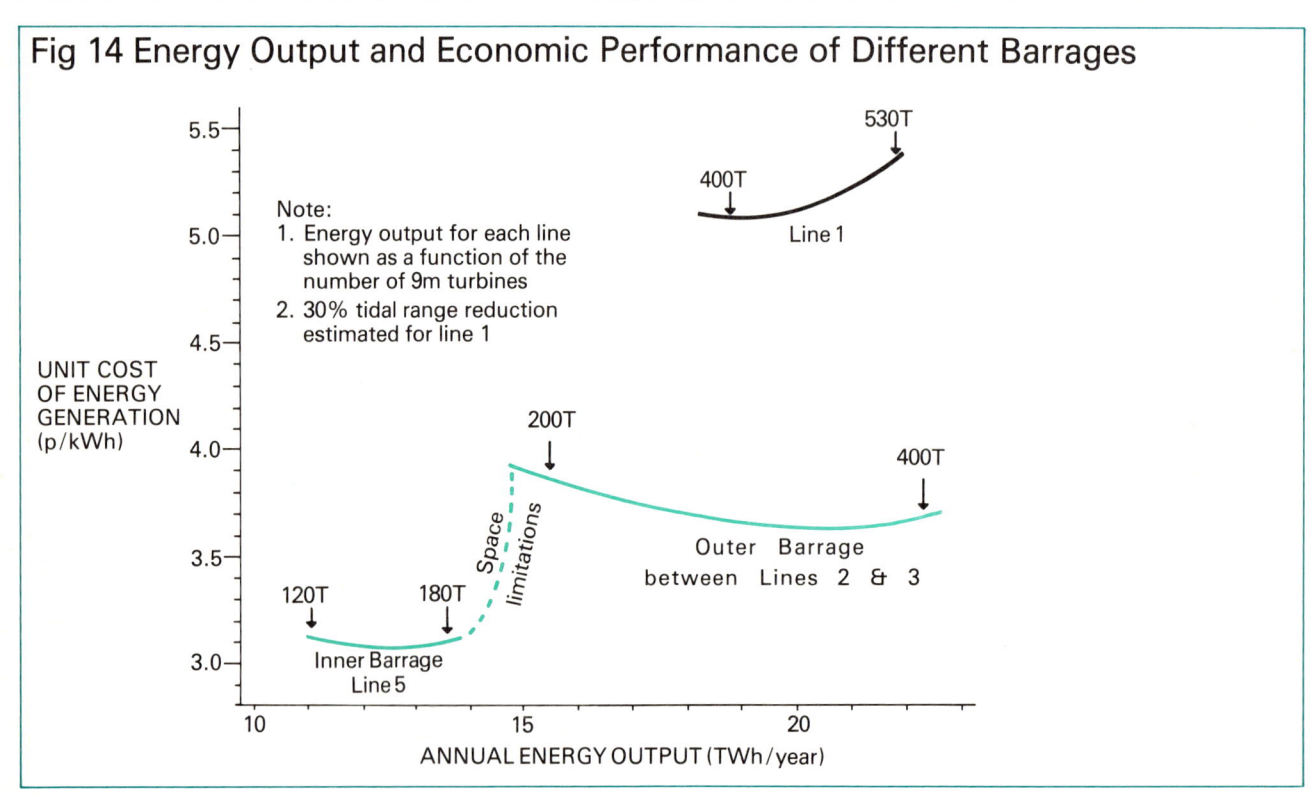

Note:
1. Energy output for each line shown as a function of the number of 9m turbines
2. 30% tidal range reduction estimated for line 1

Line 1: 400T, 530T

Outer Barrage between Lines 2 & 3: 200T, 400T
Space limitations

Inner Barrage Line 5: 120T, 180T

UNIT COST OF ENERGY GENERATION (p/kWh)
ANNUAL ENERGY OUTPUT (TWh/year)

18

The Choice of a Barrage Site   7

53. The optimum choice of a barrage depends on a large number of interacting factors. As a first step six possible lines were considered, as shown in Fig 12 opposite. The choice amongst these was initially made in terms of energy output and cost, and the favoured positions were then examined for environmental impacts in the widest sense (industrial, social, ecological, etc). In this section we deal with the energy and cost implications.

54. The factors affecting how much energy a barrage can produce are:—

(a) the head of water developed

(b) the area of the basin enclosed by the barrage

(c) the number and characteristics of the turbines, although in practice the number may be restricted by the availability of deep water.

55. The head of water developed depends on the tidal range as modified by the presence of the barrage. In addition the head depends on the number of sluices and their efficiency in permitting water flow. There is a trade-off between having enough sluices to allow the tide to reach its full height inside the barrage, and the cost of those sluices.

56. For a given number of sluices and a defined head of water, the area of the enclosed basin is the remaining major factor determining the volume of water available to drive the turbines. While barrage lines to the seaward end of the estuary generally give higher energy outputs than those further inland, the increase in energy output is less than proportional to the basin area, since the tidal range decreases down the estuary. On the other hand the wider estuary and deeper water increase the costs of the barrage.

57. The first step is to consider the maximum energy that can reasonably be extracted from various notional barrage lines. Their approximate annual energy outputs are shown in Fig 13 opposite (full line). The second step is to determine the approximate cost of building the barrage and this is shown as a dotted line in the figure.

58. The ratio of cost to energy in pence per kilowatt-hour then gives a first ranking of the various possible sites. The conclusions from this first rough assessment are:—

(a) **an Inner Barrage** in the region of line 5 would generate electricity at lowest unit cost. This reflects optimising the barrage alignment to make best use of the tidal range, the shorter and shallower crossing, and the basin area.

(b) **an Outer Barrage** between lines 2 and 3 would give the maximum energy without a steep rise in the unit cost of generation. The steep rise in unit cost westward of line 2 reflects the reduction in tidal range and the increase in length and depth of the barrage. Fig 14 shows that a barrage at line 1 would yield no more energy than a barrage between lines 2 and 3, but the unit cost of electricity generation would be a third higher.

59. Thus, while a barrage in the area between lines 2 and 3 would give the most energy, one between lines 4 and 5 would be the most cost effective. Both these areas are at obvious natural constrictions in the estuary.

60. It is now necessary to examine in more detail possible barrage schemes in the two regions between lines 2 & 3, and 4 & 5.

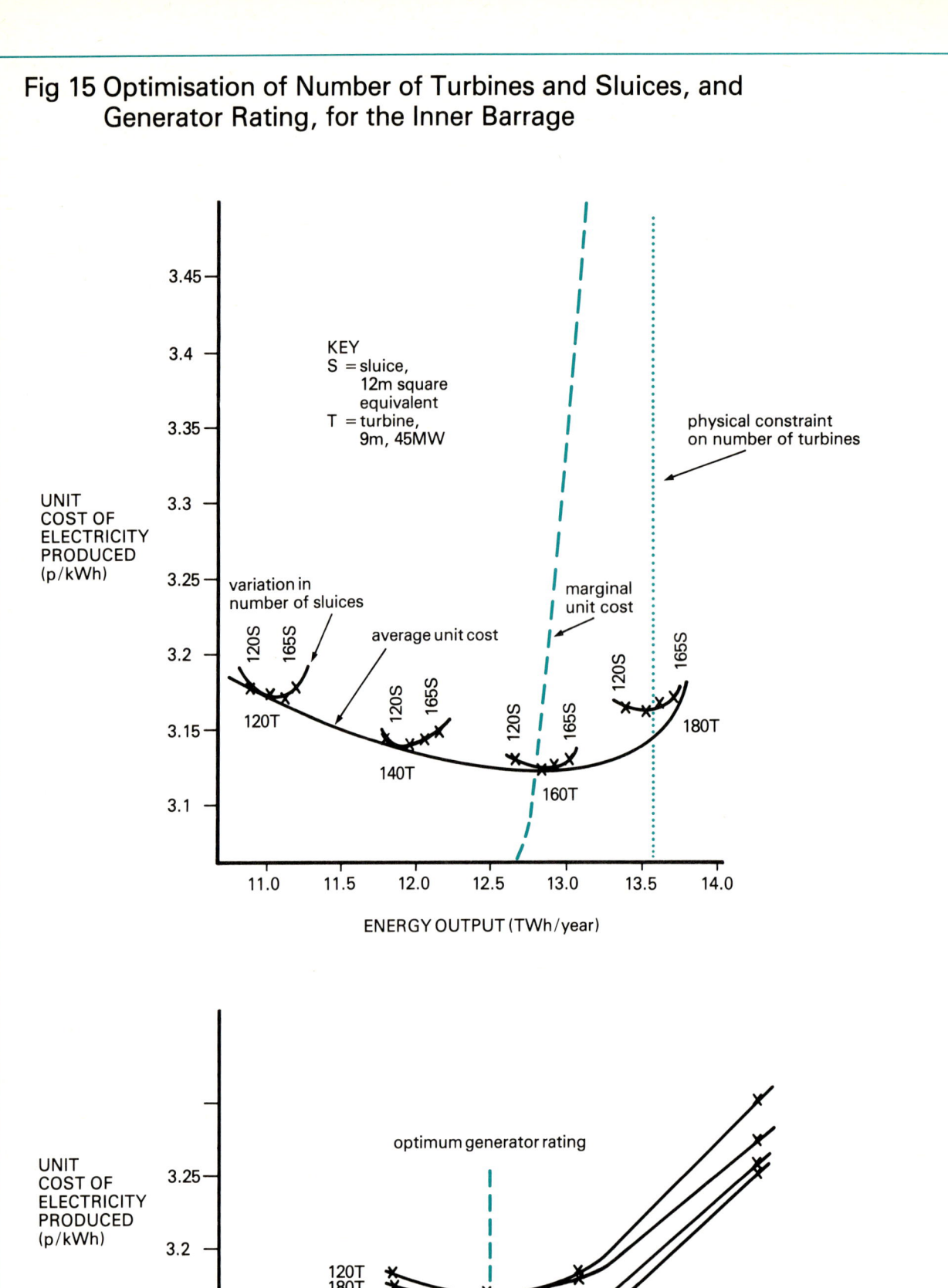

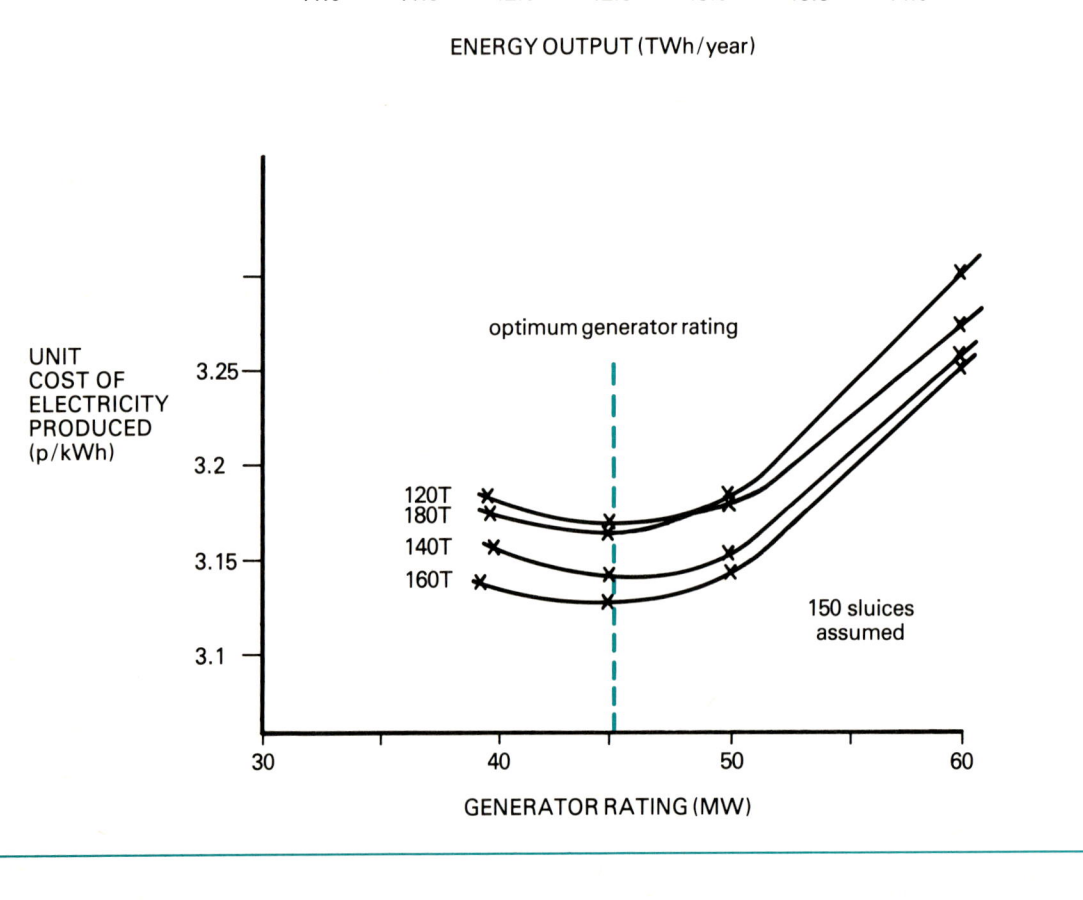

Fig 15 Optimisation of Number of Turbines and Sluices, and Generator Rating, for the Inner Barrage

Optimisation of Barrage Components and Operation   8

61. The initial choice of two possible barrage sites was based on the maximum energy output of a barrage at each of the notional lines. The next step is to optimise the various design and operational parameters for a barrage at each site. The energy output of a barrage and also its cost would depend strongly on the number of turbines and sluices which it would contain, and to a lesser extent on generator rating and turbine diameter. The energy output would also be dependent on the timing of sluice and turbine operation.

Optimisation of Numbers of Turbines and Sluices

62. Figure 15 shows a graph of the average unit generation cost in p/kWh for the Inner Barrage plotted against its energy output, which depends mainly on the number of turbines. For each different number of turbines a subsidiary curve shows how the unit cost depends on the number of sluices. The main curve is very shallow (i.e. the cost of electricity produced is not very sensitive to the number of turbines) but it has a minimum corresponding to the lowest cost electricity generation. At this point on the curve there is the possibility of choosing to install further turbines in order to obtain more energy at a higher average cost. To make this decision, the cost per kWh of the increment of energy obtainable by adding the extra turbines, (i.e. the additional cost divided by the additional energy), must be considered. This is known as the marginal cost of the additional energy. If this marginal cost, although higher than the average cost, is still less than the cheapest alternative way of generating electricity, then it would be economic to install the extra turbines.

63. The marginal cost per kWh is shown on the diagram as a broken line. The optimum number of turbines (and sluices) occurs at the point where this curve reaches the cost of the cheapest alternative supply. This is subject to the provision that the physical constraint, imposed by the maximum number of turbines which can conveniently be fitted in deep water channels, is not exceeded.

64. The precise position of the optimum depends on the cost of alternative supplies, which in turn depends on our view of the future. For example, will electricity in the future be supplied from a predominantly nuclear, or predominantly coal system, and at what fuel costs?

65. In practice the dependence of the unit generation cost on the number of turbines is not very strong in the region of interest, i.e. the average unit cost curve is very shallow near its minimum. Also, because the marginal cost curve is very steep, the optimum number of turbines is likely to be close to the number corresponding to the minimum on the average unit cost curve. The optimum number of 9m diameter turbines are estimated to be 160 for the Inner Barrage and 300 for the Outer Barrage. These figures were derived assuming that at any time only 90% of the turbines would be working.

Optimisation of Generator Rating

66. The first step in choosing the generator rating is to consider what rating would be needed to take full advantage of the energy available at the turbine during the highest tides. However, because these tides are infrequent, reducing the generator rating has a less than proportional effect on the annual electrical output. This reduction in rating would reduce the cost of the generators, the switchgear and the transmission links. An optimisation of generator size with respect to the unit cost of electricity generated has therefore been carried out. Fig 15 shows that for the Inner Barrage the optimum generator rating for a 9m turbine could be close to 45 MW. A similar study for the Outer Barrage showed this optimum to be about 40 MW. For smaller turbine diameters lower ratings would be appropriate.

Choice of Turbine Size

67. For the purpose of this study 9m diameter bulb turbines have been chosen. With a smaller turbine of proven type (e.g. 7.5m), the overall costs might be slightly more but the requirement for prototype trials could be less stringent. However, the overall economics are not unduly sensitive to this factor. A more important factor is that for the same installed capacity the use of smaller turbines would result in a slightly longer turbine block. For the Inner Barrage this physical constraint would restrict the energy output slightly to a maximum of about 12.4 TWh/year.

Optimisation of Barrage Operation

68. The energy output of a barrage is clearly dependent on how it would be operated. An adequate head of water must be allowed to develop before turbining starts and the flow rate of water through the turbines then adjusted to maximise energy output. The timing of sluice operation must similarly be optimised. Modelling studies have shown that a large starting head (4.8m for mean spring tides and 3.3m for mean neaps) would be most appropriate; this corresponds to more than half the tidal range on any given day.

69. There is also some possibility that operation of the barrage could be adjusted to amplify the natural resonance of the estuary, thereby increasing the energy output by a small amount. However, further study is required to determine what improvement in energy output could be achieved and whether the associated seiching (tidal surge) would be acceptable.

Fig 16 Leading Barrage Schemes

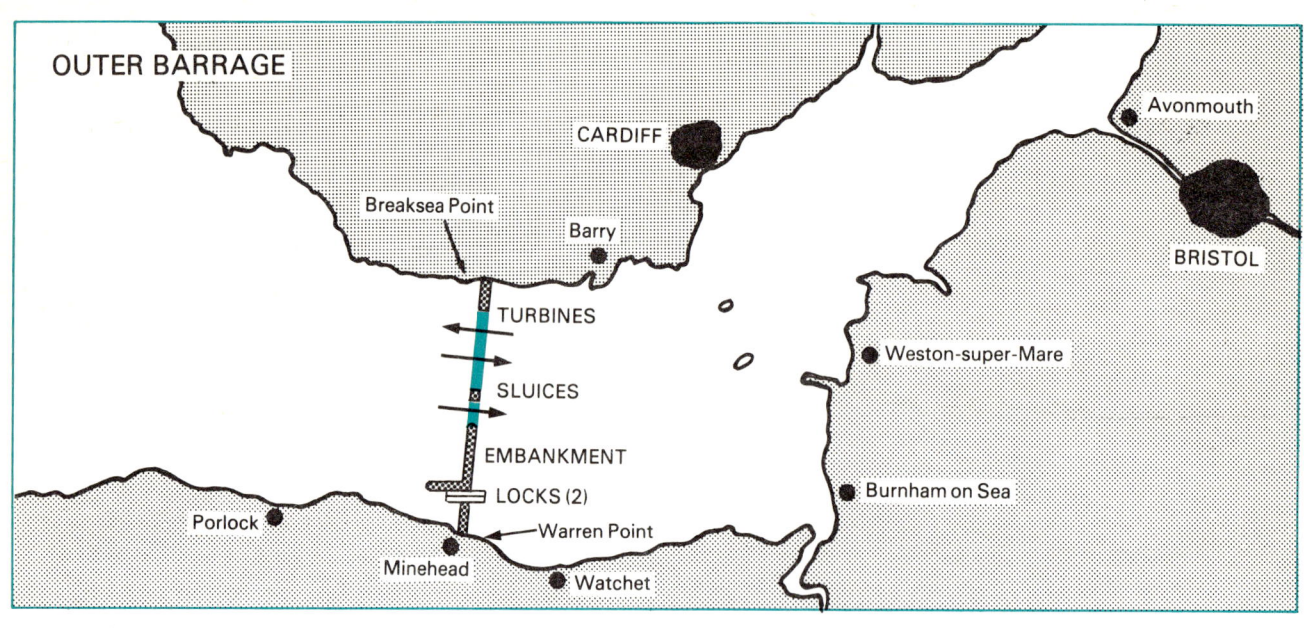

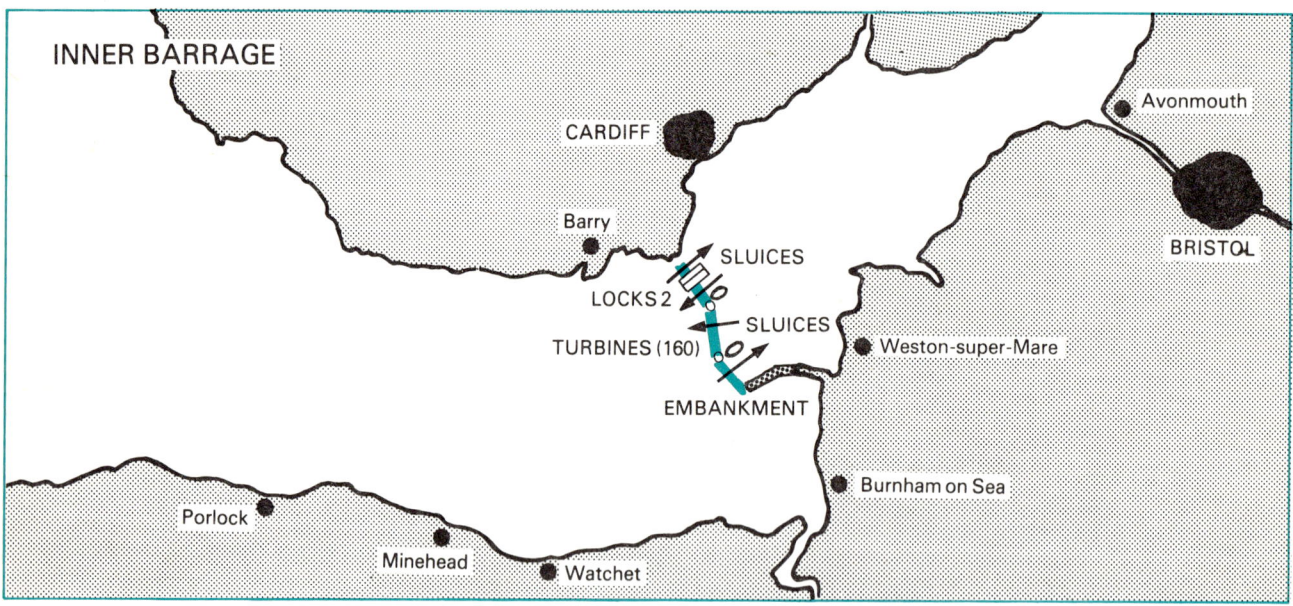

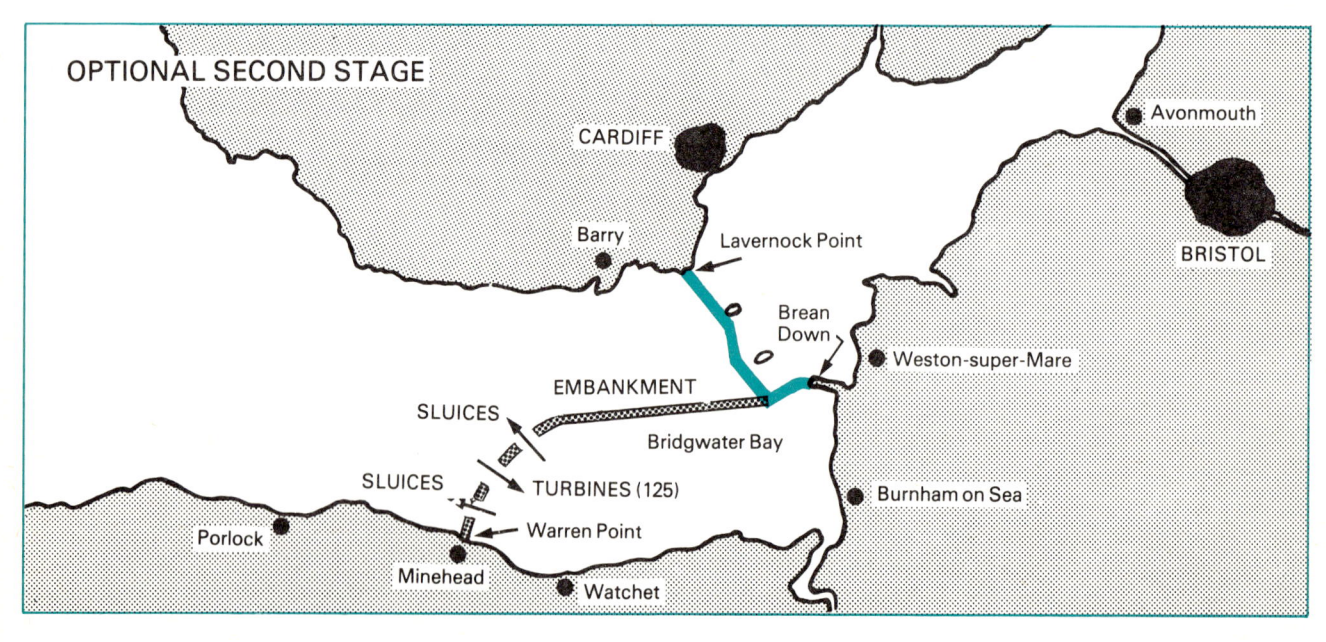

The Option of a Staged Scheme   9

70. The Committee has also considered the option of exploiting the energy potential of the estuary in two stages, as an alternative to the Outer Barrage.

71. The best Staged Scheme identified would first involve building the Inner Barrage, which would operate in the ebb generation mode. This first stage would itself be a complete scheme capable of independent operation. At any time in the future a second stage could be added. This would be bounded by a dam, branching off the Inner Barrage near Brean Down and running to just east of Minehead, enclosing Bridgwater Bay, and could operate in flood generation mode.

72. This approach has a number of attractions which stimulated its serious consideration. Firstly, capital expenditure would be spread and cash flow improved, since there would be a financial return after completion of the first stage. Both technical and financial risks would be lower than for the Outer Barrage, as there need be no commitment to the second stage until the first is complete. Experience gained in building and operating the first stage could also be incorporated in the design of the second stage.

73. Further, if the second stage were to be operated in flood generation mode, the energy output of the two stages together would be in the form of four quanta per day instead of two rather larger ones. Electricity would be generated over a longer period during each twenty-four hours than with the Outer Barrage, and could be absorbed more easily into the supply system, thus increasing its value. For the same reason the contribution of the Staged Scheme to firm generating capacity* would be greater. Also, the peak power output would be lower than with the Outer Barrage, leading to lower transmission costs.

74. Investigations have shown that the overall performance of the Staged Scheme would be generally similar to that of the Outer Barrage. Tidal modelling studies have confirmed that the Staged Scheme would generate almost as much electricity. Although the total cost of the Staged Scheme would be greater than that of the Outer Barrage, benefits would accrue earlier, as soon as the first stage started to produce power. The net effect is that the economic performance of the Staged Scheme would be similar to that of the Outer Barrage.

75. However, the economic performance of the second stage would be significantly worse than that of the first Inner Barrage stage. Thus, when considered as a separate investment decision, the second stage looks unattractive. Nevertheless, this second stage deserves mention because it shows that a decision to build the Inner Barrage still leaves the option, should later circumstances make this seem desirable, to utilise more fully the energy potential of the estuary.

*see Glossary, Annex 9

Fig 17 Electricity Storage and Tidal Power

Electricity storage in the CEGB system may be used for three main purposes:

- to store energy at off-peak times in order to meet peaks in demand at other times. This is sometimes called "peak lopping".
- to act as a standby power supply which can be switched in very rapidly.
- to help in stabilising the frequency of the alternating current in the event of major disturbances to the electrical network.

The standby and frequency control functions are usually secondary to the peak lopping and storage function except at Dinorwic. The first two of these functions can be performed either by thermal or storage plant.

It has sometimes been argued that the addition to the system of simple tidal power schemes with their variable power output, might require additional storage capacity, possibly sufficient to enable the bulk transfer of power from night to day. Such arguments lead naturally to the concept of double basin tidal schemes capable of giving a steady output during the day but importing power at night. This section examines these arguments.

DOES TIDAL POWER REQUIRE EXTRA STORAGE?

Storage is a property of the overall electricity supply system and the amount of storage must be chosen in the context of the overall system, not by having regard to one particular type of generating plant. The need for extra storage is thus decided by examining various possible ways in which the electricity supply system might develop with and without tidal power.

Analysis shows that except in the case of systems with a high proportion of nuclear power, *the introduction of tidal power would not lead to the need for more storage. Tidal power may be injected directly into the system displacing the operation of other plant.* The displaced plant will generally be fossil fuelled, not nuclear, and so the main role of tidal power would be to save fossil fuel.

It is therefore concluded that *the introduction of an ebb generation tidal power scheme into the electricity supply system does not imply the need for extra storage,* unless there is a very high proportion of nuclear plant present.

DOUBLE BASIN STORAGE SCHEMES

A tidal scheme could be designed to produce a steady power output during the day throughout the spring-neap cycle. Such a scheme would require two basins and pumping, and it would be necessary to import a similar amount of power during the night. Thus the scheme is essentially a storage scheme.

Both basins would be equipped with pump/turbines capable of turbining in one direction and pumping in the other. The main barrage could be in the region of Cardiff-Weston and would enclose the main, or high, basin. The secondary, or low, basin is enclosed by an embankment on the seaward side of the main barrage, its location being chosen to give an adequate depth. The low basin is emptied at night by off-peak pumping and the main basin is refilled by flow through the sluices and turbine passageways and/or primed at night by off-peak pumping.

During the day the turbines in each basin would be used in sequence to take advantage of the tides and produce an output of about 4000 MW over about 12 hours. There would also be some flexibility for meeting short-term peaks. The amount of power which must be imported at night is much greater for neap tides than for springs. The overall net energy output would be close to zero. It would be operated to obtain maximum benefit from the difference between day-time and night-time values of power in a system with a high nuclear plant mix.

Since this scheme is best considered as a low head storage scheme rather than an energy producing tidal power scheme, its economic performance should be compared with other storage options open to the CEGB. These include high head pumped storage, underground storage and compressed air storage.

Economic analysis of two-basin tidal storage schemes shows that about 50 GWh/day could be available at a cost of about £1900/kW, for 12 hour generation. A conservative estimate, taking into account possible environmental constraints, suggests that at least 130 GWh of equivalent high head pumped storage, including underground reservoir storage, might be available at a cost of about £970-1130/kW. *The relatively poor economic performance of two-basin storage schemes therefore rules them out as a storage option.*

The benefit/cost ratio of two-basin schemes is considerably worse than that of an ebb generation scheme. *Thus a two-basin storage scheme does not provide the most cost effective way of developing the estuary as an energy resource.*

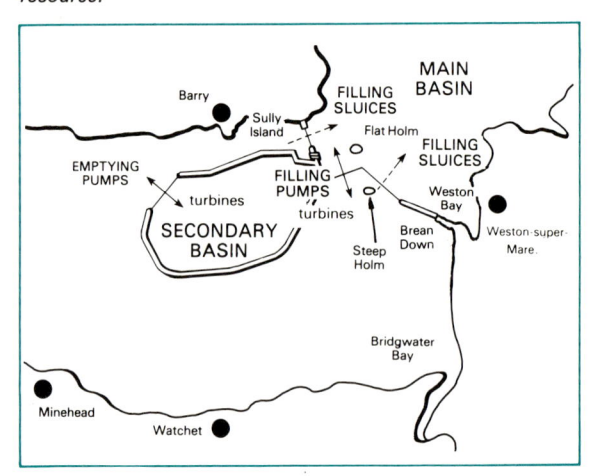

DOUBLE BASIN SCHEMES FOR GENERATION WITH STORAGE

An important variant on the two-basin scheme with pump/turbines is to remove the constraint that the day-time energy output should remain constant over the spring-neap cycle. In this unconstrained scheme the second basin is used mainly to retime much of the power output of the main basin, thus producing firm power by day, although the level of firm power varies from 2250 MW at neap tides to 4500 MW at spring tides. Power is imported at night, especially around neap tides, to complete emptying of the second basin. However, the amount of power imported is much lower than for the pure storage scheme and so this scheme is a net producer of energy, producing almost as much energy per year as an ebb generation scheme. Essentially, however, its operation involves an element of storage dedicated to the tidal power scheme and as we have seen, storage in the estuary is relatively expensive.

The benefit/cost ratio of this unconstrained scheme, although better than that of the two-basin storage scheme, is still significantly worse than that of the best ebb generation schemes. Thus, unconstrained two-basin schemes are not a cost-effective way of developing the Severn Estuary as an energy resource.

The Possibility of a Second Basin for Storage   10

76. As already discussed, the electricity output from a barrage would depend on the tidal range (which varies over the month) and upon the timing of the flood and ebb tides each day. Although the Staged Scheme would allow generation for a longer period each day, there would still be times when the barrage would generate when the energy is least needed (e.g. during a night-time trough in demand).

77. It has been suggested that at such times the electricity generating system might not readily be able to absorb the output of the tidal scheme, particularly if only "inflexible" baseload nuclear plant were available to be displaced. To avoid wasting the tidal energy at such times a two-basin scheme could be designed and built to store energy at night and generate by day. This would be achieved by using the tidal electricity generated during a demand trough to empty the second basin. The resulting head difference between the water in this basin and the sea would be used subsequently to regenerate the electricity when it was required.

78. Alternatively, both the main basin turbines and the second basin turbines could be designed to pump in the direction opposite to generation, when required, so that energy could be stored in both basins. By raising the level of the main basin at night and at the same time emptying the second basin, regular amounts of energy could be provided for about twelve hours each day. The ratio between energy output and input varies from springs to neaps and overall is close to one. This type of scheme is therefore best considered as a pumped storage scheme* which uses the tides to obtain an operating efficiency of around 100%.

79. Detailed analysis of these possibilities has led to the conclusion that energy storage in the Severn Estuary is likely to be at least twice as expensive as alternative ways of providing that storage. Typical alternatives are high-head storage of the type commonly associated with Dinorwic, or underground storage. The advantages of storage are essentially within the context of the total national electricity generation system and there is no particular advantage in linking it with any specific generating plant, including a tidal scheme.

80. It has been suggested that in the future sites for high-head storage might be restricted, and that the viability of alternative storage options has not yet been proven. However, even in these circumstances energy storage in the Severn Estuary is unlikely to be economically attractive.

81. Moreover, there could also be severe environmental objections to a two-basin energy storage scheme in the estuary, because there would only be one tide a day in the main basin, in which the water level would remain close to or even above the present high tide level throughout the night. This could have strong adverse impacts on many areas such as land drainage, sea defence and the ecosystem, including birds.

*Note: The storage application of a second basin should not be confused with the use of a second basin for power generation as part of the Staged Scheme discussed earlier.

Fig 18 Costs of Leading Barrage Schemes

Cost Item	Approximate Uncertainty	Inner Barrage 160 T$_2$, 150 S	Outer Barrage 300 T$_1$, 320 S	Staged Scheme I: 160 T$_2$, 150 S II: 125 T$_1$, 100 S
	%	£M	£M	£M
Locks	± 20	300	235	350
Embankments	± 20	530	825	1,995
Caissons (turbine, sluice & blank)	± 10	1,650	2,500	2,560
Turbines	+ 15 − 30	970	1,815	1,730
Transmission	± 10	500	925	780
Prototype Trials	+ 20 − 40	165	165	165
Miscellaneous	−	105	150	150
Engineering Overheads	−	305	485	570
Contingency & Post Tender Costs	−	1,135	1,760	2,120
TOTAL CAPITAL COST	+ 6 − 10	5,660	8,860	10,420
Annual Maintenance	−	35	60	65

T$_1$ = no. of 9 m 40 MW turbo-generators
T$_2$ = no. of 9 m 45 MW turbo-generators
S = no. of 12 m square sluice equivalents

Note:
1. Costs are in December 1980 prices.
2. Interest during construction is not included in these costs, but this factor has been taken into account in the economic analysis presented later.
3. Estimates of uncertainty in cost, which are only approximate, were provided by the Committee's engineering consultants.

The Cost of a Barrage 11

82. The construction of a Severn Barrage would be a massive financial undertaking involving the expenditure of several billions of pounds. In addition to direct construction costs there would be some indirect costs arising from the various impacts of the barrage on man and the environment (see later). In the time available it has only been possible to quantify some of these in financial terms. However, the preliminary judgement of the Committee is that the total of quantifiable indirect costs is unlikely to exceed 5-10% of direct costs. Indirect costs would also be partly offset by indirect benefits. Direct construction costs therefore dominate the economic evaluation.

Direct Construction Costs

83. The table opposite shows the breakdown of construction costs for possible configurations of the three leading barrage schemes. Although these costs are subject to some uncertainty, they are in general based on a conservative engineering approach and rely where possible upon established technology. The Committee considers that some savings should be possible when the design of major components is considered in more detail.

(a) Turbo-generators and Transmission

84. The mechanical and electrical components of a barrage could together account for around one-third of total barrage costs. The uncertainty in turbine costs is relatively large since there is little experience of manufacturing machines of diameter as large as 9m, especially for operation in exposed marine conditions. The costs presented assume the use of bulb turbines. Recent studies now indicate that these costs might be reduced by up to 25%, including an allowance for volume production techniques. If this should be the case, total barrage costs would be reduced by 6%. There is also some indication that the use of less proven technologies (e.g. rim-generator) might enable turbine costs to be further reduced by 20-30% and associated caisson costs by 10-15%.

(b) Caissons

85. Turbine, sluice and blank caissons also constitute about one-third of total costs. Although present designs are only preliminary, they are based on accepted design standards for normal reinforced concrete. Thus, the uncertainty in their costs is thought to be relatively small. The largest uncertainties in this area relate to the placement and foundation of caissons, but these factors might constitute only about 3-5% of total barrage costs.

(c) Embankments

86. Embankments would account for only about 12-15% of the cost of a simple ebb generation barrage, although this proportion would rise significantly for the second phase of the Staged Scheme. Although there is considerable experience of embankment construction, cost estimates can vary widely, being very dependent on the cost of large rock. However, should embankment costs turn out to be larger than expected, embankments in deep water could be replaced by blank caissons.

(d) Locks

87. Ship locks constitute only 7-8% of total costs although they might seem expensive in absolute terms. The uncertainty in costs arises from doubt about the length of breakwater which might be required.

The Cost of a Barrage (Continued)

Maintenance

88. The barrage is assumed to have a nominal working life of 120 years (although in practice it could be much longer), with all plant and equipment being replaced every 40 years. The annual cost of normal operation and maintenance is estimated to be at most 1% of the capital cost of plant and equipment and 0.75% of the cost of the structure.

Overheads, Contingencies and Post Tender Costs

89. A 7% engineering overhead on all costs has been added to cover final design, detailed site investigation, model tests and supervision of construction, in accordance with normal UK engineering practice.

90. An allowance for contingencies, amounting to 10% of civil engineering costs and 5% of turbine and transmission costs, has been made. However, no allowance had been included for the risk of escalation in real costs resulting from unforeseeable delays in the construction programme, e.g. arising from industrial disputes.

91. Finally 17½% of total costs has been added on the recommendation of CEGB to cover post tender cost increases, other than those due to inflation, including increases due to escalation in construction timescale and design change. This totals £800M for the Inner Barrage and suggests the need for the design of barrage elements to be well developed before tenders are sought. Meanwhile this forms an additional contingency.

92. The large number of turbines needed for a barrage make prototype trials desirable for the detection of potential type faults. Such trials would be essential if unproven plant were to be chosen. They should also reduce post-tender costs. Similar arguments apply to trials of caisson founding and placement.

Indirect Costs

93. Assessment of the costs of various impacts of a barrage is described later. Many of these indirect costs have not yet been quantified. Those so far costed are:
- **Water quality in the Estuary.** Capital costs of £120-230M for additional effluent treatment works, with an annual running cost of £12-24M, might be incurred. The need for this expenditure would depend on future policy decisions regarding water quality standards.
- **Land Drainage.** Capital costs of £14-19M could be incurred.
- **Sea Defence.** Improvements to sea defences might cost up to £10M.

94. Costs arising from possible modification of trade to the ports has not yet been quantified, but would depend markedly on the scheme chosen, being least for the Inner Barrage.

95. Many impacts of a barrage on the natural environment are intrinsically unquantifiable in financial terms.

96. Indirect costs would to some extent be offset by indirect benefits e.g. to employment and recreation. The former is difficult to quantify a decade or so in advance, but could be substantial. The barrage could also promote recreation by boosting tourism and giving rise to a new marine leisure industry. The social benefits of improved recreation to health and enjoyment, though unquantifiable, could be important.

97. An early consideration of the allocation of responsibility for meeting consequential costs and paying for consequential benefits is required if the acceptability of a barrage is not to be prejudiced. If, as would seem equitable, these costs are considered an integral part of the costs of the barrage, its benefit/cost ratio could worsen by up to 0.07.

Fig 19 Schematic Annual Load Duration Curve, Illustrating Plant Merit Order for a Generating System without a Barrage

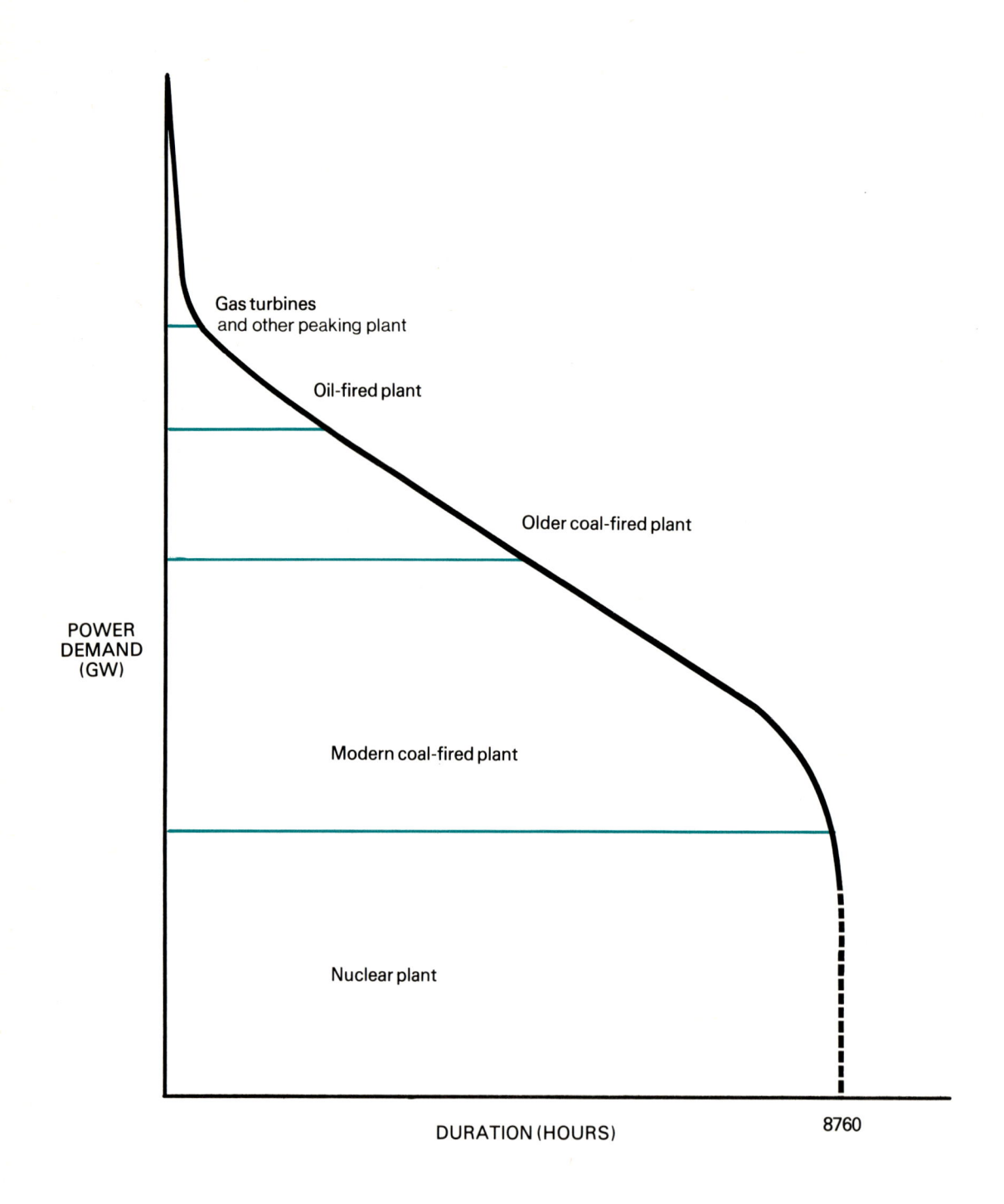

POWER DEMAND (GW)

- Gas turbines and other peaking plant
- Oil-fired plant
- Older coal-fired plant
- Modern coal-fired plant
- Nuclear plant

DURATION (HOURS) 8760

Note
For illustrative purposes the average available capacities of different types of plant have been superimposed on the demand curve on this diagram. In fact, plant availabilities are not constant throughout the year. Also, the level of available capacity for each type of plant will depend on the scenario being considered.

The Economics of Tidal Power   12

98. The next question to be considered is whether the cost of a tidal barrage can be justified by the benefits to be derived from it, i.e. the economic evaluation of such schemes. In this section, only the economic performance of a barrage as a producer of electricity is considered. The ecological, social and industrial benefits and disbenefits, which might also arise, are set aside for discussion later.

99. The unit cost of generating electricity from an Inner Barrage, based on current best estimates of the cost of constructing and operating the barrage and of its energy output, is about 3.1 p/kWh. There is, of course, considerable uncertainty surrounding the cost estimates used, but current expectations are that the generating cost will be within 0.5p of this figure. This is broadly comparable with the expected generating costs of other types of plant in the year 2000, as shown in Fig 20. The generating costs shown include both capital and operating costs, but no allowance has been made for the differences in firm power contribution, which are low for tidal but high for other types of plant.

100. To determine whether tidal electricity at this cost is economically attractive, it is now necessary to compare the cost of producing it with its value within the national electricity generating system.

101. The demand for electricity varies from hour to hour throughout the year and is met by a mix of types of generating plant, each of which has its special role within the system. Once a certain mix of plant is installed in the system, decisions about how to operate it are based on the *avoidable operating costs* of the various types of plant. For conventional plant, these costs will be dominated by fuel costs. To meet demand at a given time, plant will be brought on stream in reverse order of its avoidable operating cost, i.e. in its proper position in the so-called *merit order.* Plant with low operating costs (e.g. nuclear) is used to meet the base load, while plant which combines low capital cost with high operating cost, such as gas turbines, is used at a rather low annual load factor to meet peaks in demand. This is illustrated in the schematic load duration curve shown in Fig 19.

102. The benefits of various possible tidal power schemes must now be evaluated within the context of the electricity supply system and then compared with those of alternative investment options.

103. A tidal scheme, once constructed, would have very low avoidable operating costs and would therefore be used as an energy source whenever possible. By far the most important benefit would therefore be the net saving in total system operating costs. This saving is the reduction in generation costs of thermal power stations displaced from operation (i.e. those of the highest avoidable cost that would otherwise be operating at the time) less the small direct operating costs of the tidal scheme. Until the proportion of nuclear plant in the generating system reaches a high level, these savings would mainly consist of savings in the cost of fossil fuel.

104. In contrast, a barrage would make only a relatively small contribution to the overall requirement for power stations, which are required so that the demand should always be met with a defined level of security. Because the output of a tidal barrage would be intermittent, its contribution to the system operating capacity required would only be typically 15% of its own nominal installed capacity.

105. *Thus, the principal effect of building a barrage would be to save fuel in thermal power stations rather than to reduce the need to construct other power stations.*

Fig 20 Costs of Electricity Generation in the Year 2000

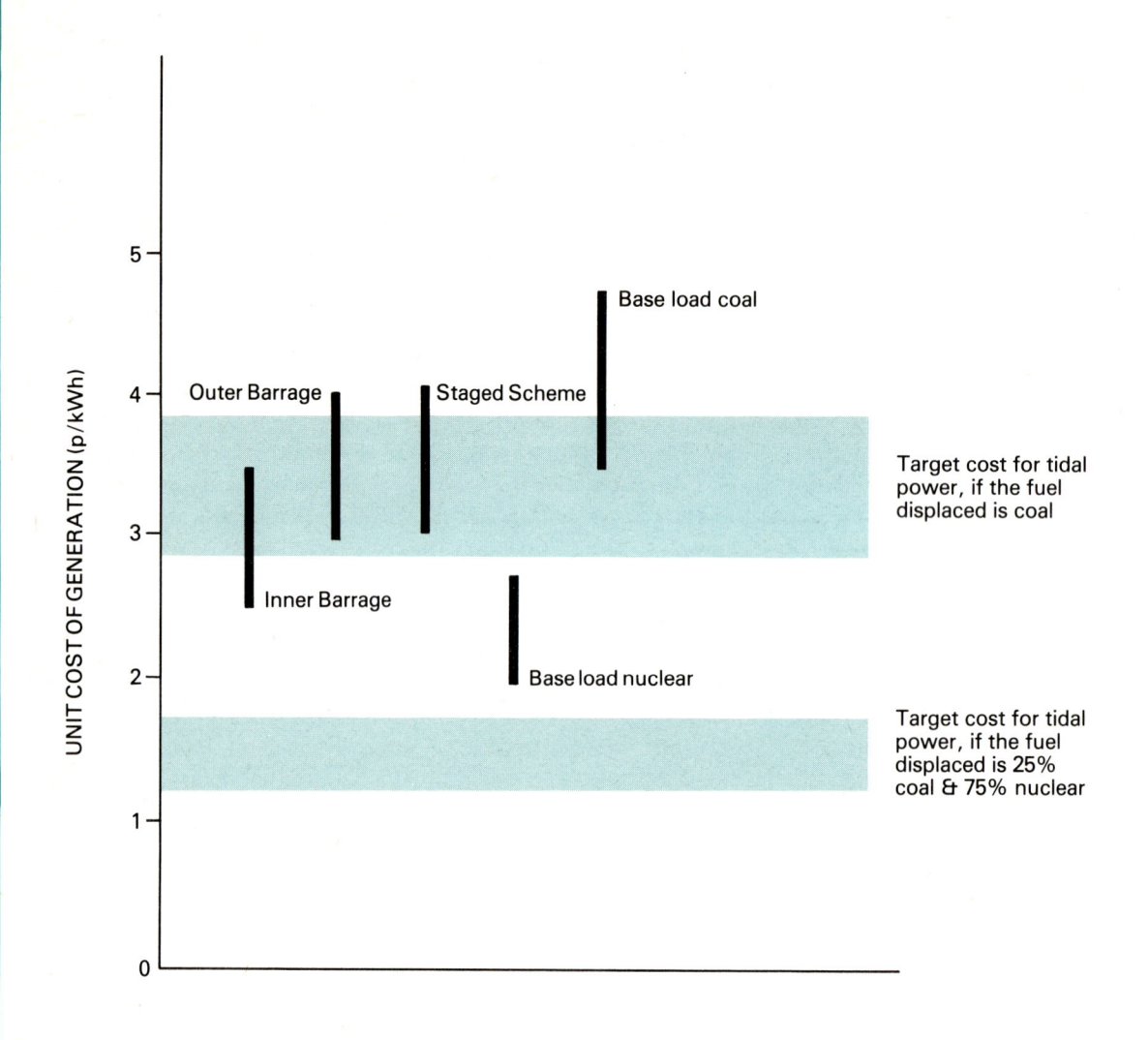

UNIT COST OF GENERATION (p/kWh)

- Outer Barrage
- Inner Barrage
- Staged Scheme
- Base load coal
- Base load nuclear
- Target cost for tidal power, if the fuel displaced is coal
- Target cost for tidal power, if the fuel displaced is 25% coal & 75% nuclear

Notes:

(a) All costs are shown in December 1980 money values.

(b) Coal and nuclear costs are based on those in the lower case of the Department of Energy's "Energy Projections 1979", expressed in December 1980 money values.

(c) The range shown about the central value is in each case ± 15%.

(d) The target cost for tidal power when only coal is saved assumes a coal cost of 34p/therm and a thermal efficiency for coal fired plant of 33%.

(e) The target cost for tidal power, in a generating system in which the fuel saved is 75% nuclear and 25% coal, assumes a nuclear fuel cost of 9p/therm and a thermal efficiency for nuclear plant of 33%. Such a system could probably not be reached until well into the next century.

The Economics of Tidal Power (Continued)

106. Both the capital cost and the operating savings of a tidal barrage are large. Because the firm power credit is small, it is a useful approximation in a preliminary examination of tidal economics to set aside the firm power contribution and consider whether the estimated net operating savings of a tidal scheme exceed its capital costs. In Fig 20 the generation costs of various tidal barrages, expressed in terms of p/kWh, are compared with crude values of fuel savings, expressed as target costs. On this basis some tidal schemes might be economically attractive in systems where coal dominates fuel savings, but would probably not be viable against a background in which the proportion of nuclear plant in the generating system rises rapidly.

107. However, this is an oversimplified form of analysis which gives no more than a crude indication of the economic performance of tidal power. The analysis is confined to a single year and to one set of assumptions and excludes any allowance for differences to firm power credit. Another disadvantage of this simple approach is that it ignores the possibility of changes in the mix of generating plant that would subsequently be installed if a tidal barrage were to be present in the system.

The Total System Model

108. For these reasons the main economic evaluation of tidal power in this study has been based on a computerised model of the whole generating system. This is a modified version of the Department of Energy's investment model of the electricity supply industry for England and Wales. In addition, sub-models have been developed at Harwell to incorporate the effects of tidal power and of storage on electricity demand. A full description of the structure and operation of the models and of the results obtained is given in Chapter 13 of Volume 2.

109. For any level of electricity demand the model determines the optimum mix of plant (subject to whatever constraints are imposed) and calculates the total systems cost (operating and capital) of meeting demand. The value of the benefits arising from a tidal barrage is determined by first calculating the cost of meeting electricity demand without tidal power under a certain set of conditions. Then, the output of the barrage is subtracted from the original electricity demand and the cost of meeting the residual demand from the non-tidal system is computed. The benefit of the barrage to the system is then the difference between these two costs. This benefit can then be compared with the cost of the barrage in a benefit/cost ratio. Similarly, the model can be used to study the benefits arising from other types of investment, e.g. in nuclear plant, so that comparisons can be made between the available options. In addition the sensitivity of the results to variation in the assumptions made can be explored.

110. The model takes no account of the additional costs of "cycling" other plant (i.e. bringing it into or out of operation rapidly) which would be incurred when a tidal barrage is present. It therefore tends to overstate the benefits of tidal power slightly (see para. 115).

Fig 21 Installed Capacity of the Electricity Supply System in Different Scenarios

	Year:	1980 GW	2000 GW	2010 GW	2020 GW	2030 GW
Scenario I						
Nuclear		5.1	27.9	50.9	68.3	75.0
Coal		43.0	30.5	25.5	25.9	31.2
Oil		9.2	11.8	9.8	—	—
Gas turbines and other peaking plant		3.4	7.9	6.8	11.8	13.0
		60.7	78.1	93.0	106.0	119.2
Scenario II						
Nuclear		5.1	16.3	21.8	25.0	25.0
Coal		43.0	42.1	54.6	68.8	81.1
Oil		9.2	11.8	9.8	—	—
Gas turbines and other peaking plant		3.4	8.0	6.8	12.3	13.1
		60.7	78.2	93.0	106.1	119.2
Scenario III						
Nuclear		5.1	27.9	41.0	68.7	72.6
Coal		43.0	28.6	25.5	13.5	18.0
Oil		9.2	5.4	—	—	—
Gas turbines and other peaking plant		3.4	7.9	10.8	11.6	12.0
		60.7	69.8	77.3	93.8	102.6

Notes

(a) All numbers have been rounded

(b) In Scenario I the proportion of nuclear plant rises from 36% to 63% over the period 2000 to 2030 whereas in Scenario III it rises from 40% to 71%.

The Economics of Tidal Power (Continued) RESULTS

111. The economic viability of a barrage must be judged largely in terms of the cost savings arising from the fuel it displaces. It will therefore depend strongly upon the assumptions made about the price and mix of fuels used to generate electricity. To arrive at reasonably robust conclusions it is therefore useful to look at the economics of tidal power in a number of different scenarios, or views of the future.

112. Broadly it turns out that the benefit/cost ratio of a barrage is around 1. Whether this ratio is above or below 1 depends on the assumptions already referred to and illustrated in the various scenarios considered. However, it is predicted that an alternative investment in nuclear plant would yield a significantly higher return in all these scenarios.

Future Scenarios

113. The following three main scenarios have been considered. Since the future is sufficiently imponderable that none of them can necessarily be regarded as more probable than any other, these scenarios are intended to provide a broad quantitative framework for consideration of possible energy futures and policy choices. They do not imply Government commitment to particular levels of energy production or plant mixes. While none of these scenarios is a prediction of what will happen or is a prescription of what should happen, it may be noted that Scenario III is similar to the one presently adopted by the CEGB for planning purposes.

Scenario I
A higher demand, slightly constrained nuclear view of the future, similar to the lower case of Energy Projections 1979 (Dept. of Energy). Gross domestic product grows at an average annual rate of 1.8% over the next 50 years. Electricity demand (GW) rises gradually at an average annual rate of 1.8% to 2000 and 1.3% from 2000 to 2030. New nuclear planting is constrained to a maximum of 3 GW per year after 2000. A projection of coal prices on the international market has been used to reflect the national opportunity cost of using coal, the values* being 34p/therm in 2000 rising to about 40p/therm in 2030.

Scenario II
A higher demand, low nuclear view, in which nuclear planting is constrained to 1 GW per year from 1990. All other assumptions are as for Scenario I.

Scenario III
A low demand, unconstrained nuclear view, similar to that being used by the CEGB for planning purposes, in which electricity demand grows more slowly than in Scenario I and the proportion of nuclear plant in the system rises rapidly. Electricity demand grows at average annual rates of 1.2% to 2000 and 0.8% from 2000 to 2030. There is no restriction on the rate of nuclear construction post 2000, other than the requirement for new plant. Higher oil prices than are used in Scenarios I and II cause oil fired power stations to be phased out of use rapidly after 2000. For the purposes of this study the same coal prices as in Scenario I have been used, although the CEGB planning view would usually be based on UK prices for coal. (UK coal prices* are assumed by CEGB to be around 26p/therm in 2000, rising to about 40p/therm by 2030. If UK coal prices should fall below international prices, the benefit of a barrage to the CEGB would be less than its benefit to the nation.)

Fuller details of the assumptions of these scenarios can be found in Annex 5. The plant mix calculated by the model for each scenario is shown in Fig 21.

---

*For consistency, these prices are shown in terms of the value of money in December 1980. These figures are 32% higher than when expressed in March 1979 money, which was the base used throughout the economic evaluation.

Fig 22 Comparison of an Inner Barrage with Nuclear Power

	Benefit/Cost Ratio	
	Inner Barrage	Additional nuclear power (4 GW)
Scenario I	1.10	2.00
Scenario II	1.40	2.30
Scenario III	0.95	1.55
Scenario I — but with 3% discount rate	1.60	2.20
Scenario I — but with 7% discount rate	0.75	1.75
Scenario II — but with reduced availability of nuclear plant, (a).	1.40	1.85

(a) 60% average annual availability of nuclear plant, as compared with 70% in Scenarios I and II

Note: Figures rounded to nearest 0.05

The Economics of Tidal Power (Continued)

Benefit/Cost Ratio

114. In each of the scenarios, a benefit/cost ratio has been calculated for the leading barrage schemes. This ratio is that of the total discounted benefits arising from the barrage (i.e. the reduction in discounted system cost of the rest of the electricity supply system) to the total discounted costs of its construction (see Annex 6). A discount rate of 5%, representing the opportunity cost of capital, is used in the calculations, this being the rate of return presently required by Treasury for public investment. A benefit/cost ratio which exceeds unity indicates that the project yields more than the required 5% rate of return and is therefore economic in this sense.

Results for the Inner Barrage

115. Results for the Inner Barrage in various scenarios are shown in Fig 22. No allowance has been made for the increased costs of cycling thermal plant when a barrage is introduced. It has been suggested that this factor might reduce benefit/cost ratios by about 6%. However, the need for increased cycling of other plant could be reduced to some extent by varying the barrage output over short periods, with little effect on total energy output.

116. Fig 22 shows that the benefit/cost ratio of the Inner Barrage could fall within the range 0.95-1.4 in the three main scenarios, indicating that the Inner Barrage would meet or would be close to meeting the required rate of return. The barrage would be most attractive if the future rate of nuclear construction is low (1 GW/year, Scenario II). The barrage would be least attractive if the proportion of nuclear plant in the generating system rises rapidly, particularly if total electricity demand grows relatively slowly (Scenario III, demand growth 0.8% per year from 2000).

117. However, it is also necessary to ask whether there is any other type of investment in the electricity supply system which would yield a better return. Fig 22 compares the Inner Barrage with the construction of an additional 4 GW of nuclear power stations between 1990 and 2000, an investment which would involve a similar level of capital expenditure. In all these scenarios the nuclear investment would give a better benefit to cost ratio.

118. The comparison of tidal with nuclear power in any given scenario is influenced by all the assumptions made. For example, as the proportion of nuclear plant in the generation system rises, the benefit/cost ratio of new nuclear plant falls as shown in Fig 22 (see also Annex 6). This figure also shows the effects of different discount rates and of a lower assumption about nuclear plant availability on the results. Although both low discount rates and lower plant availability narrow the gap between tidal and nuclear power, the conclusion remains that investment in nuclear plant, provided it is an available option, is preferable to investment in an Inner Barrage.

119. There may of course be constraints on nuclear investment (e.g. public concern over safety, the availability and acceptability of suitable sites, the capacity of the nuclear construction industry) which might mean that nuclear investment is not an available option on the scale required. In addition, uranium supply could become a problem in the medium to long term, and the cost, availability and acceptability of fast reactors are not yet established. If such considerations as these turn out to be important, the Inner Barrage could be an economic alternative.

Fig 23 Comparison of Tidal Schemes

Scenario	Benefit/Cost Ratios				
	Inner Barrage	Outer Barrage	Staged Scheme	Second Stage of Staged Scheme	*Outer Barrage minus Inner Barrage
Scenario I	1.10	0.90	0.95	0.65	0.60
Scenario II	1.40	1.25	1.15	0.70	0.90
Scenario III	0.95	0.85	0.80	0.55	0.70

Notes

(a) Figures rounded to nearest 0.05

(b) *Benefit/cost ratio representing the return on the additional investment required for the Outer Barrage, over that required for the Inner Barrage.

The Economics of Tidal Power (Continued)

Breakdown of the Benefits

120. Before going on to consider other possible barrage lines, it is interesting to note the way in which the benefits of the Inner Barrage arise. The dominant element in the total discounted benefit is savings in the cost of fuel burnt in other power stations. For example, in Scenario I this accounts for 80% of the total benefit. The remainder of the benefits arise from capital cost savings (15%) and savings in non-fuel operating costs (5%).

121. The pattern of fuel saving varies over time in a manner dependent on the scenario, and benefit/cost ratios in the various scenarios are very much influenced by this pattern. For example, in Scenario III the absence of oil savings adversely affects the benefits of tidal power, whereas the dominance of coal savings (and absence of low-value nuclear savings) in Scenario II results in a relatively high value for the benefit. Fig 25 shows the composition of total fuel savings in energy terms over the first 30 years of barrage operation. However, it must be remembered that savings in the early years of operation, which would have a greater fossil fuel component, would have a greater weight in the total discounted value of benefits than those occurring later.

122. The second, less important, benefit from a tidal barrage is its contribution to the firm capacity required to meet demand at a given level of system security. An approximate estimate of this benefit is provided in the system as the difference between the installed capacity requirements with and without the barrage, once the pattern of investment has settled down. A more accurate estimate would require a detailed probabalistic analysis. In the case of an Inner Barrage in the reference Scenario I, the installation of 7.2 GW of tidal capacity leads to net savings of about 1.1 GW in other plant. This is made up of a reduction of 1.4 GW in the requirement for coal fired plant* together with a small increase (0.3 GW) in the requirement for gas turbines. The latter requirement is not unexpected, since the presence of a tidal generator in the system will tend to increase the peakiness of the load on thermal plant.

Other Barrages

123. The main alternatives to the Inner Barrage are an Outer Barrage, which would make fuller use of the energy potential of the estuary, and a Staged Scheme in which the Inner Barrage would be followed by a bund enclosing the Bridgwater Bay area and operating in the flood generation mode. The Staged Scheme would produce about as much energy as an Outer Barrage, but its timing would be more evenly distributed throughout the day. It also has the advantage that some of the expenditure can be delayed until after the first stage is generating.

124. Fig 23 compares these schemes with the Inner Barrage for each of the three scenarios. In all cases, the Inner Barrage emerges as the most attractive economically. The Staged Scheme and the Outer Barrage must be considered marginal except in the low nuclear scenario, II. However, when the second stage of the Staged Scheme is considered as a separate investment, the *additional* investment involved would be uneconomic. Similarly, if one considers the return on the *additional* investment which would be required to build the Outer Barrage instead of the Inner Barrage, this also would be uneconomic.

Sensitivity of Tidal Economics to Assumptions Made

125. A study of risk and sensitivity in the economics of tidal power has shown that the main areas of sensitivity of the above results are:
- delays in the barrage construction programme
- delays in turbine manufacture, installation and commissioning
- the value to the generating system of the energy produced
- the quantity of energy produced by the barrage.

---

*By comparison, the current phase of Drax coal-fired station has an installed capacity of 2 GW.

Fig 24 Sensitivity of Tidal Economics to Coal Price Assumptions in Scenario I

| | Coal Price Assumption p/therm || Benefit/Cost Ratio ||
	Year 2000	Year 2030	Inner Barrage	Outer Barrage
High	45.9	52.1	1.20	1.05
Reference	34.3	39.3	1.10	0.90
Low	29.7	33.0	1.00	0.85

The use of different coal costs leads to a small change in plant mix, which slightly reduces the effect on the benefit/cost ratio of the change in coal costs.

Coal prices are in pence/therm for internationally traded coal, shown in December 1980 money values.

Benefit/cost ratio rounded to nearest 0.05.

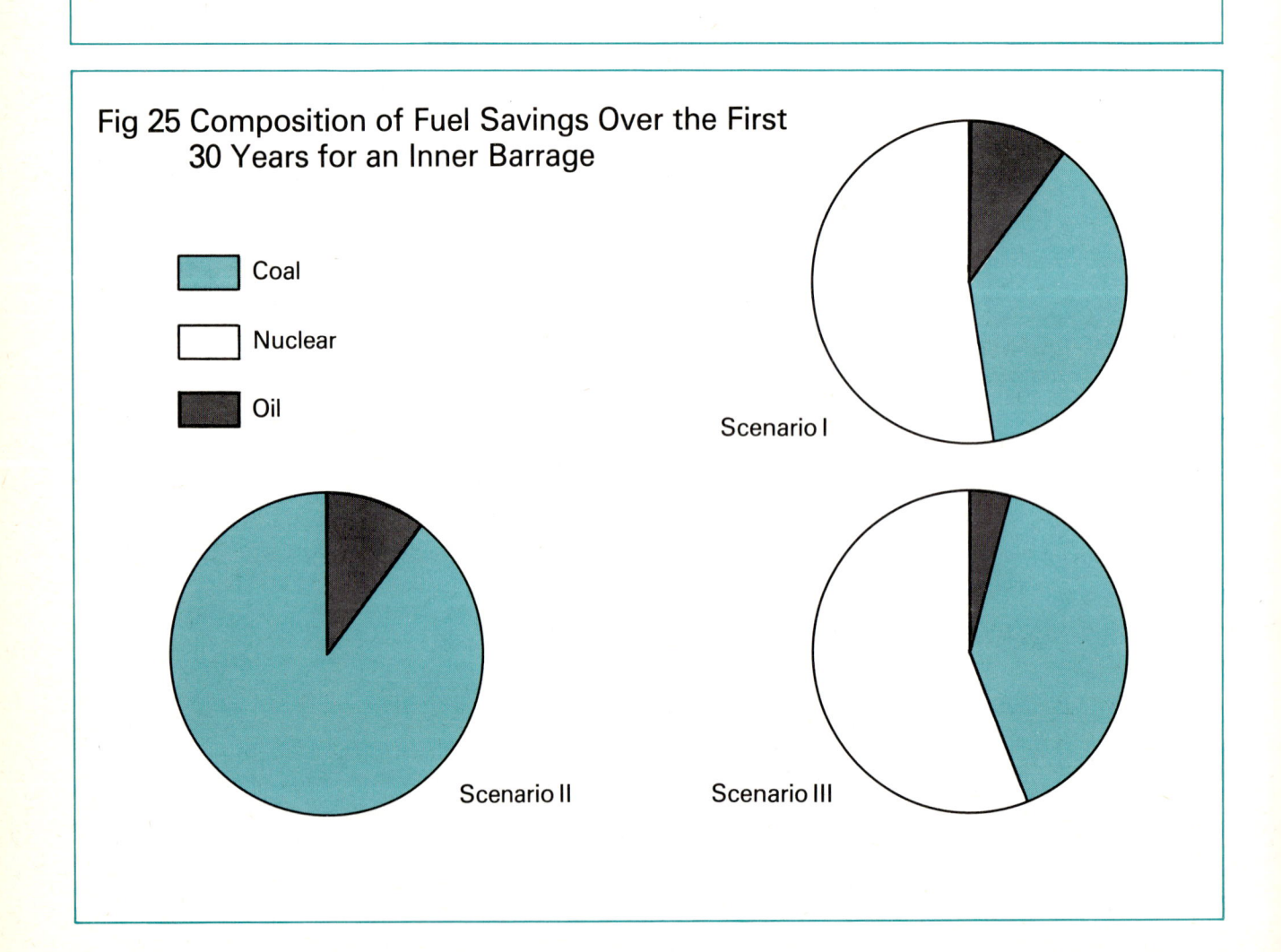

Fig 25 Composition of Fuel Savings Over the First 30 Years for an Inner Barrage

- Coal
- Nuclear
- Oil

Scenario I

Scenario II

Scenario III

The Economics of Tidal Power (Continued)

126. The greatest area of economic risk has been identified as arising through possible delays in construction. High calibre project management would be required to minimise this risk. Detailed consideration of how the construction programme should be managed would be required in any future study.

127. The first two areas of sensitivity listed above affect costs and the last two influence benefits. Clearly the benefit/cost ratio is sensitive to the total capital cost. However, this ratio is more sensitive to delays in construction than to uncertainties in individual items of cost. Also, because the future is uncertain and we are looking a long way ahead, the uncertainty in benefits is greater than the uncertainty in costs.

128. An important difference between the leading barrage schemes is that the economic viability of the Inner Barrage (i.e. the probability that benefits will exceed costs when both are discounted at 5% a year) is much less sensitive to how the future may turn out than that of either the Outer Barrage or the Staged Scheme.

129. The system has also been used to investigate the sensitivity of tidal economics to some of the factors affecting the value to the electricity generating system of the tidal energy which is produced. Results, relating mostly to Scenario I and the Inner Barrage, are presented in Chapter 13 of Volume 2.

130. The most important findings is, as expected, that higher coal prices raise the benefit/cost ratio, whereas lower coal prices reduce it (Fig 24). However, oil prices also influence the total benefit considerably, since most oil saving occurs in the earlier years of barrage operation. If oil prices are assumed to move in parallel to coal prices, then the effect of oil and coal price rises together on the benefit/cost ratio in Scenarios I and II would probably be about twice as great as that shown in Fig 24. On the other hand, in Scenario III, rising oil prices are assumed to lead to earlier phasing out of oil fired plant and hence would have less effect on tidal economics.

131. Another important observation is that a lower rate of growth of electricity demand would reduce the attraction of tidal power, as illustrated by the difference in benefit/cost ratios for Scenarios I and III (Fig 22).

132. However, such changes in fossil fuel prices or electricity demand would have a similar effect on the benefit/cost ratio of an alternative investment in nuclear plant.

The Effect of Pumped Storage on Tidal Power Economics

133. The role of energy storage, in providing a means of regulating fluctuations in supply and demand, has been described earlier.

134. It has sometimes been suggested that, because large pulses of tidal energy would frequently become available at periods of low demand, these might with advantage be "retimed" by the use of pumped storage and made available at a time of high demand, when the value of fuel savings would be greater.

135. Only a limited treatment of storage has been possible in this study because the investment model used does not optimise pumped storage as part of the system. However, tentative results indicate that the presence of various levels of pumped storage capacity in the electricity supply system would make very little difference to the total benefits obtainable from a barrage in any of the scenarios examined.

136. The preliminary conclusion is, therefore, that little or no additional investment in storage plant would be necessary in order to take full advantage of a tidal power scheme as a fuel saver.

Fig 26 Summary of Impacts of a Tidal Barrage

CAUSES
- Changes in water levels
- Changes in water flow patterns and velocities
- Changes in sedimentation patterns
- Physical presence of the barrage

IMPACTS ON MAN
- Impact on Ports and Navigation
- Recreational Opportunities
- Impact on Amenity
- Impact on Industry
- Impact on Employment
- Opportunity for an Estuary Crossing
- Impact on Land Drainage and Flooding
- Impact on Agriculture
- Impact on Sea Defences
- Impact on Water Quality in the Estuary

IMPACTS ON THE ENVIRONMENT
- Impact on Birds
- Impact on Migratory Fish
- Impact on Marginal Wetlands
- Impact on the Balance of the Estuarine Ecosystem
- Impact on Geological Sites

Fig 26 Summary of Impacts of a Tidal Barrage

Impacts on Man and the Environment   13

137.   Any tidal power barrage would produce impacts on such diverse areas as navigation to the various estuary ports, recreation and amenity, employment and various elements of the environment particularly the estuarine habitats affecting birds and migratory fish. Some of these would be somewhat different for each of the possible tidal schemes.

138.   The various impacts and their causes are to a large extent inter-related and many complex issues are involved. The answers to these questions require relatively long term studies or information not yet available, e.g. on details of sediment patterns with a barrage present, and there are therefore a number of remaining uncertainties. Thus the conclusions reached on environmental impact are inevitably less certain than those reached on technical feasibility and economic acceptability. Also, it is not possible or indeed desirable to quantify some impacts in economic terms.

139.   The aims of the pre-feasibility study have been limited to:
- identifying any ecological, social and industrial impacts which might rule out all schemes or particular schemes or modify existing schemes
- making a start on studies to fill gaps in the basic data, especially those with a long lead time
- reaching initial conclusions on the various potential impacts, both beneficial and adverse, on the basis of the best information available
- identifying work required in any future study to establish the environmental acceptability of a Severn Barrage.

140.   Most of the potential impacts arise from the effect that a tidal power scheme would have on tidal range and hence water velocity, salinity, dispersion of pollutants, water flow patterns, sediment movement etc. There would also be some impacts due to the physical presence of the barrage. Not only would parts of the estuarine habitats be directly affected by the construction, e.g. seabed and landfall sites, but there would also be some obstruction to important migratory fish including salmon, eels and shad.

141.   The following sections describe the various impact assessments starting with the basic causes for many of them, the most important of which are changes in water levels, water flow and sedimentation patterns.

Fig 27 Examples of Water Level Changes in Different Parts of the Estuary Following Construction of the Inner and Second Stage Barrages

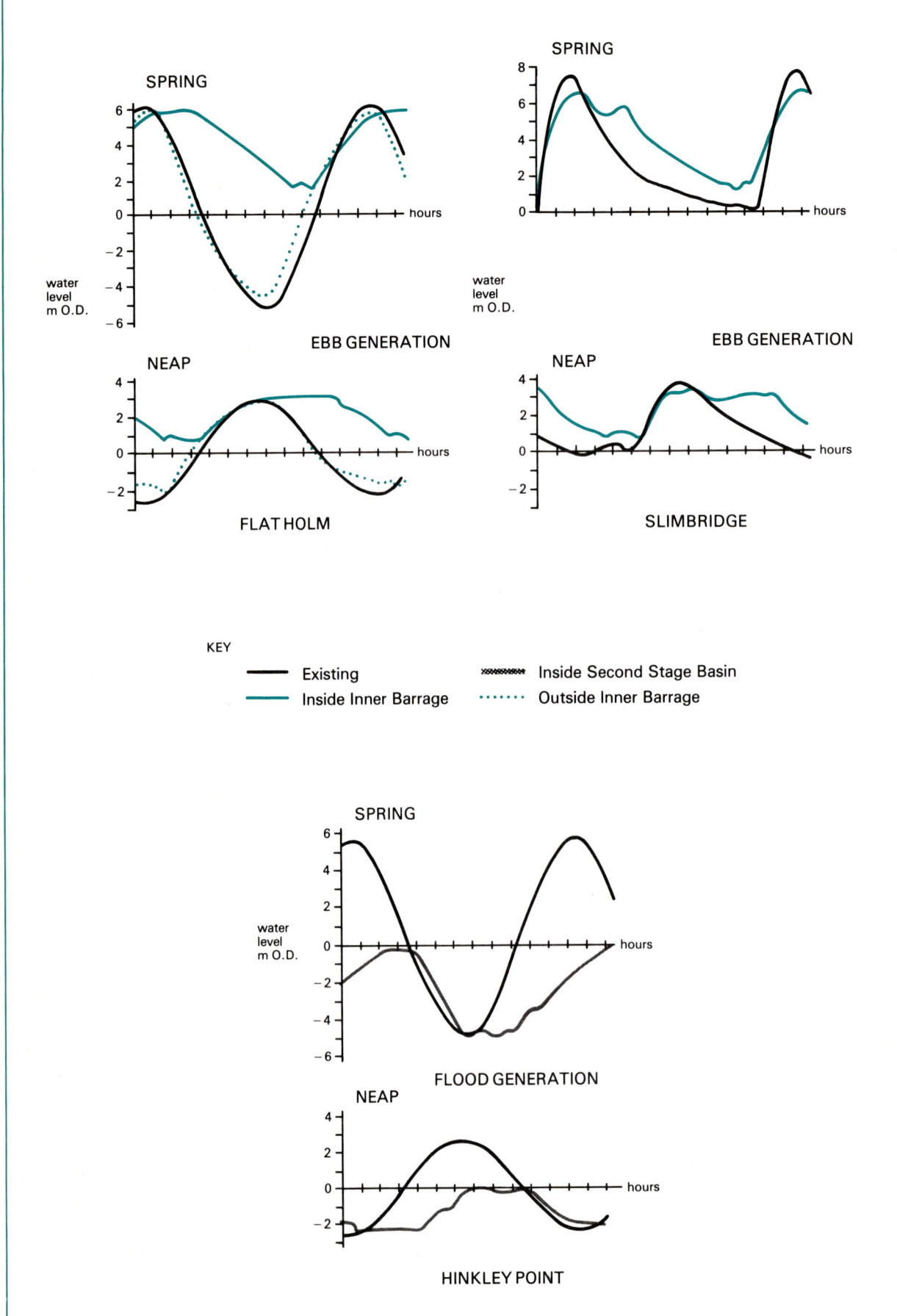

Water Levels 14

142. Changes in water levels:
- determine the energy which could be extracted from a barrage
- influence navigation and the drainage of low lying land
- could lead to major recreational and amenity benefits above a barrage
- would alter the exposure of the present foreshore and inter-tidal banks. This would affect the habitat of large numbers of wading birds and wildfowl.

143. The tidal range to seaward of a barrage would be reduced as explained earlier. Numerical model predictions indicate that immediately outside the Inner Barrage there would be a reduction in mean tidal range of about 11%, while for the Outer Barrage there would be a 20% reduction. The Staged Scheme would show a 24% reduction in mean tidal range at the Stage I barrage and a 15% reduction at the seaward end of the Stage II barrage. There would, however, be some scope for modifying these effects by optimising the operation of sluices and turbines in the two basins.

144. In the basin behind the barrage the water levels would also depend on the type of scheme and the way in which it might be operated. For example:
- in an ebb generation scheme the water levels in the basin would vary roughly between present mid-tide level and just below present high tide
- in a flood scheme the basin water level would vary between present mid-tide and present low water.

145. Fig 27 shows the water levels close to the barrage for both ebb and flood generation schemes. The water level ranges within the basins would correspond roughly to the average tidal range around the UK coast but, as this figure shows, the tide curve would be rather complex. This is because the variation of tidal levels would be determined by the operating characteristics of the barrage. There would be a period of typically two hours at spring tides and five hours at neaps when the basin level is held constant before turbining commences.

146. For ebb generation the extended period of high water, which is held prior to the start of power generation, leads to the foreshore being covered for longer periods than would occur with natural tides. Reductions in foreshore exposure would be most noticeable at places such as Weston-super-Mare where the lower part of the beach is nearly flat.

147. The precise shape of the tide curve depends on the detailed dynamics of the water movement in the basin. This results in an extended period of high water at sites near the barrage, as illustrated opposite for Flatholm, but near the head of the estuary there would be a double high tide, as shown for Slimbridge.

Accuracy of Predictions

148. The widespread effects of changes in water level mean that it is important to know how accurately new water levels can be predicted. The discrepancy between the results of the various tidal models and the real tides in the estuary without a barrage is very small, being only 2-3% of the tidal range. Any assessment of the probable accuracy of tidal range predictions with the barrage present is more complicated. Possible errors arising from the way the models represent the various components and method of operation of the barrage have not yet been estimated. However, modelling experts consider that changes in water levels following construction of a barrage can now be predicted to within ±0.2m for the Inner and Outer Barrages, but with slightly lower accuracy for the Staged Scheme.

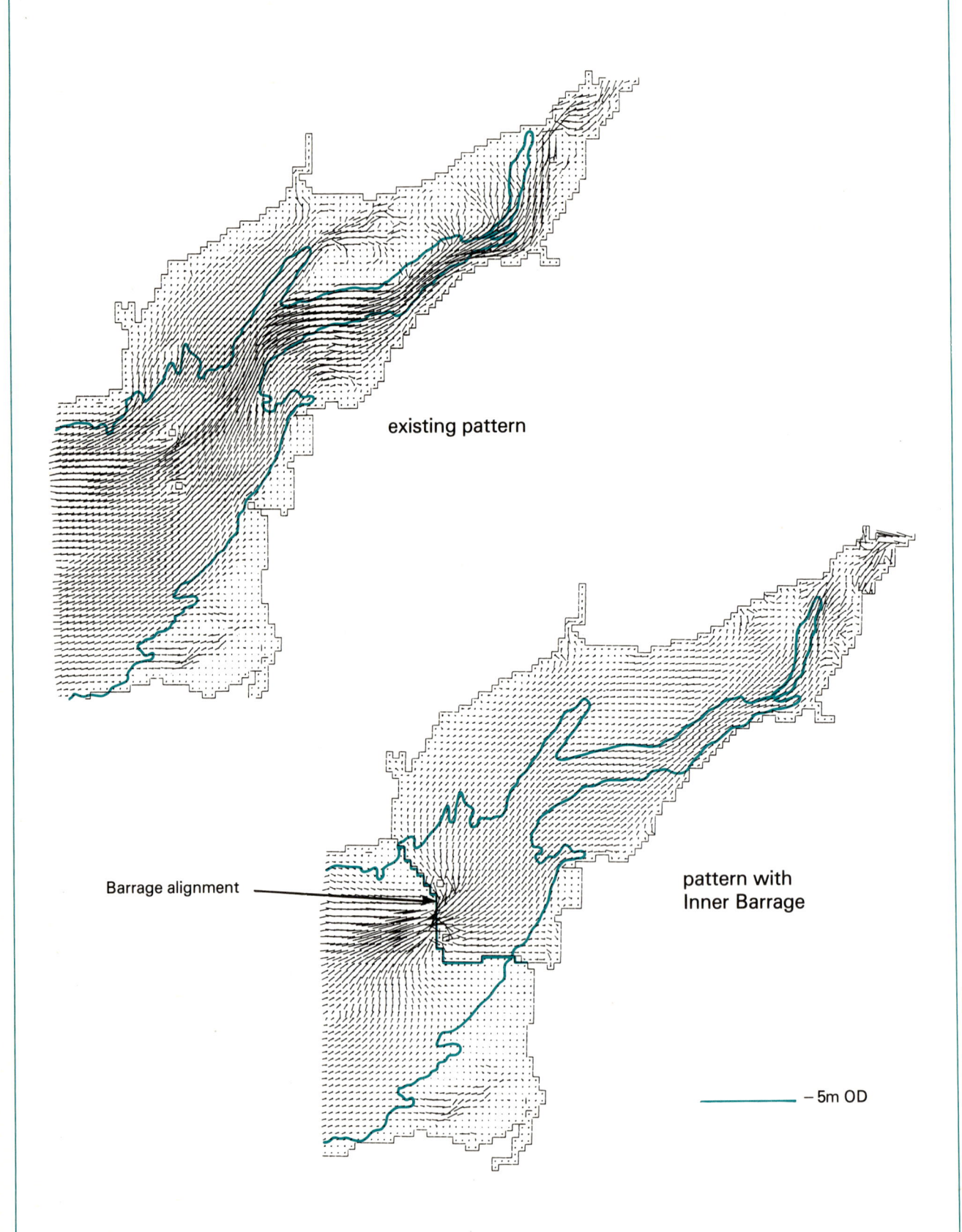

Fig 28 Water Flow Patterns on the Ebb Tide, for the Inner Barrage

existing pattern

Barrage alignment

pattern with Inner Barrage

——— −5m OD

Tidal currents on the falling tide (5.3 hours after high water), for the existing situation and for the Inner Barrage with all turbines on load

Flow Patterns 15

149. Changes in water velocity and flow patterns are important because they would affect the sediment load carried by the water and sedimentation patterns. These in turn could have important implications for navigation and the natural environment. Also, dispersion of pollutants would change and this could have industrial impacts as well as affecting the environment.

150. The presence of a barrage would affect the pattern of water movement in several ways:

- the flow pattern would change as construction of the barrage progresses
- water velocities would in general be significantly reduced behind the completed barrage, due to the reduction in tidal range
- similar reductions in water velocities to seawards of the barrage would also occur, the effects diminishing with distance from the barrage
- the flow pattern would be modified because the barrage would constrain flow to the turbine and sluice passageways at predetermined times.

151. In an ebb generation scheme between 75% and 80% of the flood tide flowing into the basin would enter through the sluices. The remaining inflow would pass through the turbines which would idle in reverse. All of the outflow would pass through the turbines.

152. Since the turbines are likely to be in a single block in the deepest water in any scheme, the outflow would be a single strong flow. The sluices would be in the next deepest water in two or more blocks and so the inflow would be made up of several flows spread out across the estuary. These stream flows would spread out, ceasing to be evident 10 km or so from the barrage.

The Inner Barrage

153. A two dimensional numerical water movement model of the estuary has been used to compare flow pattern with and without the Inner Barrage. Fig. 28 shows the strengths and directions of currents for an average ebb tide, 5.3 hours after high water. The main results are:

- currents in the basin would not be concentrated to the same degree in the deep water channels. This is because less of the basin would have drained out by this time, resulting in a greater overall water depth.
- the pattern of flow would concentrate towards and then diverge from the working turbines. The strongest currents would be well aligned with existing flow directions.
- only a small zone extending a kilometre or so either side of the turbines and sluices would have a stronger current regime than at present. In the remainder of the estuary, currents would be gentler.
- flow patterns in Bridgwater Bay would remain essentially unchanged.

Fig 29 Surface Sediments in the Severn Estuary

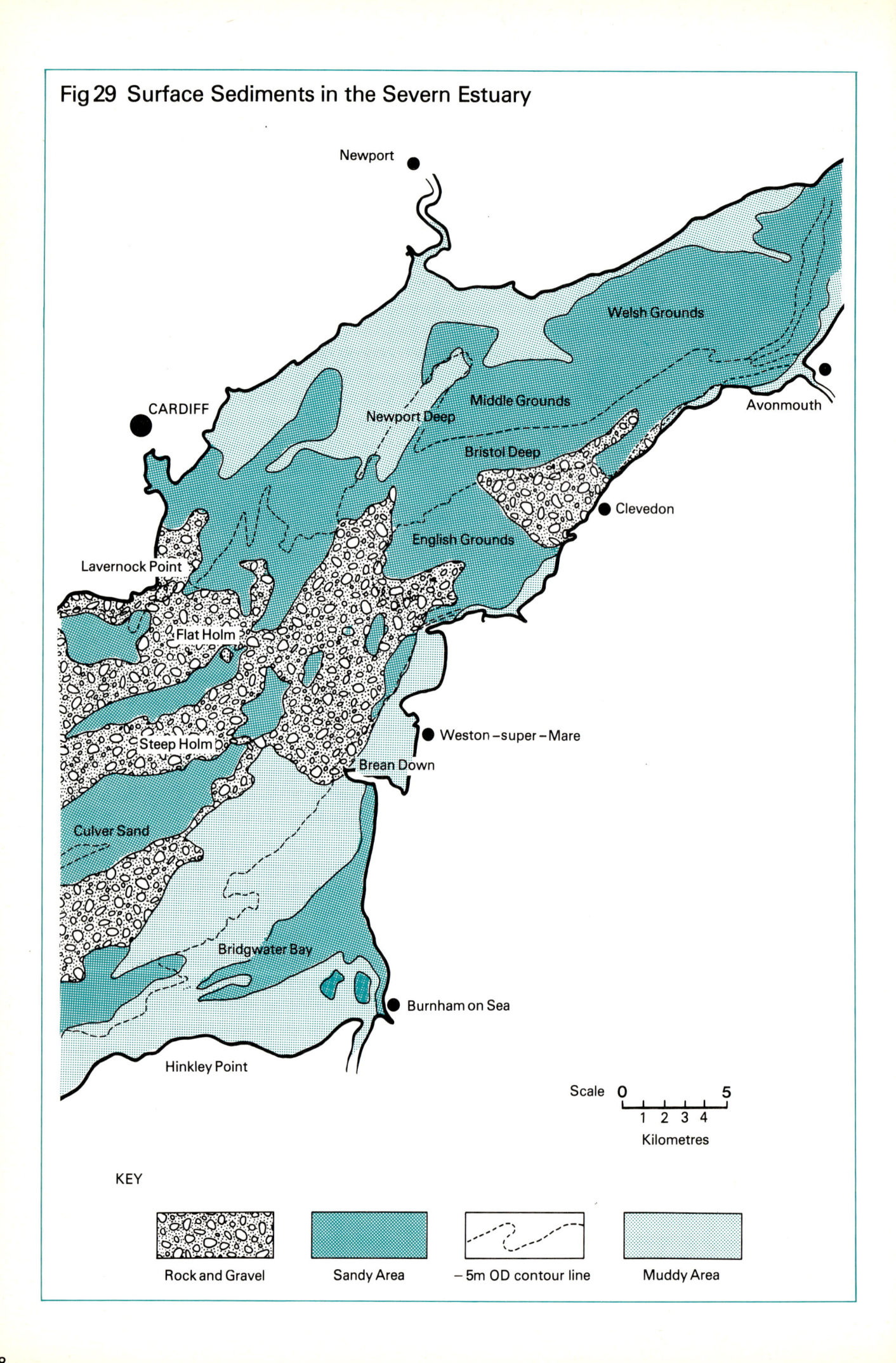

KEY

Rock and Gravel | Sandy Area | –5m OD contour line | Muddy Area

Sedimentation   16

154. Changes in the pattern of sediment transport, deposition and erosion in the estuary could result in a wide range of possible impacts. Among those requiring investigation are:

Scheme performance. Could sediments be deposited in or near the sluices and turbine waterways or cause erosion of turbine runners and other vulnerable parts of the barrage?

Navigation. Would additional dredging be necessary to maintain navigation channels?

Land Drainage and Flood Protection. Would siltation of river and stream channels discharging into the Severn upstream of a barrage be caused by raised water levels in the estuary, to the detriment of land drainage and flood evacuation?

Pollution. Some sediments may contain noxious substances. Would redistribution of these be damaging if scour mobilised them?

Marine Biology. Would reduction in the present high turbidity of the water and consequent increased light penetration result in algal growth increasing on occasion to nuisance proportions, with consequent reduction in oxygen concentration? Would the increased light penetration increase the mortality of bacteria significantly, benefiting water quality? Would there be changes in the type of sea bed, e.g. covering of an area of hard rock by sediments, resulting in changes in colonisation by plants and animals?

Inter-tidal ecosystem. Would existing areas of the upper foreshore be eroded and new ones created? If so, would such changes affect the area of marginal vegetation and the distribution of invertebrates with consequent effects on the numbers and distribution of wading birds and wildfowl?

Tentative Predictions

155. The factors which govern sediment movement are extremely complex. Work so far has been concentrated on understanding the present pattern of sediments and factors governing their behaviour. Data from the water movement model has been used to predict bed stress and other parameters relating to sediment transport. These, combined with data on the distribution and behaviour of existing sediments have enabled the following preliminary and tentative judgements to be made concerning the effect of a barrage on sediment movements:

- The generally reduced tidal velocities above and immediately below the barrage would cause settling out of a significant portion of the present suspended sediment load. This is in limited supply, despite the large amount currently mobilised in spring tides.
- The general pattern of sediment movement in the inner estuary could continue to be dominated by circulations generated by existing flood and ebb channels. It is not yet clear whether the gentler regime will lead to a reduction in dredging requirements. Although average sand transport rates could be significantly reduced, local effects might be important.
- Dredged navigational approaches to the new locks in the barrage might require maintenance dredging because of the influx of mud.
- Scour near the turbine and sluice exits could keep them free of sediment. However, the high velocities in these limited areas might mobilise local surface deposits more than at present.
- Some adjustment to the alignment and location of sluices and turbines might be needed to avoid localised problems of scour, e.g. in Bridgwater Bay during construction.
- Changes in water flow patterns would lead to changes in the pattern of accretional and erosional areas. Accretional zones are likely to be further seawards but rates of accretion are likely to be lower.
- The overall spatial variability of bed character is likely to be maintained but there would be detailed local changes.

156. Because of the complexity and uncertainty in this area extensive further work would be required in any future study. This would include numerical model studies relating to sediment transport, and a physical model to provide detailed information on water movements, both supported by further data collection. The lack of firm predictions on sediment movement is causing considerable uncertainty at this stage in predicting the impact on ports and the natural environment.

Fig 30 Duration of Water Level Above Specific Heights for Cardiff at Mean Spring Tides

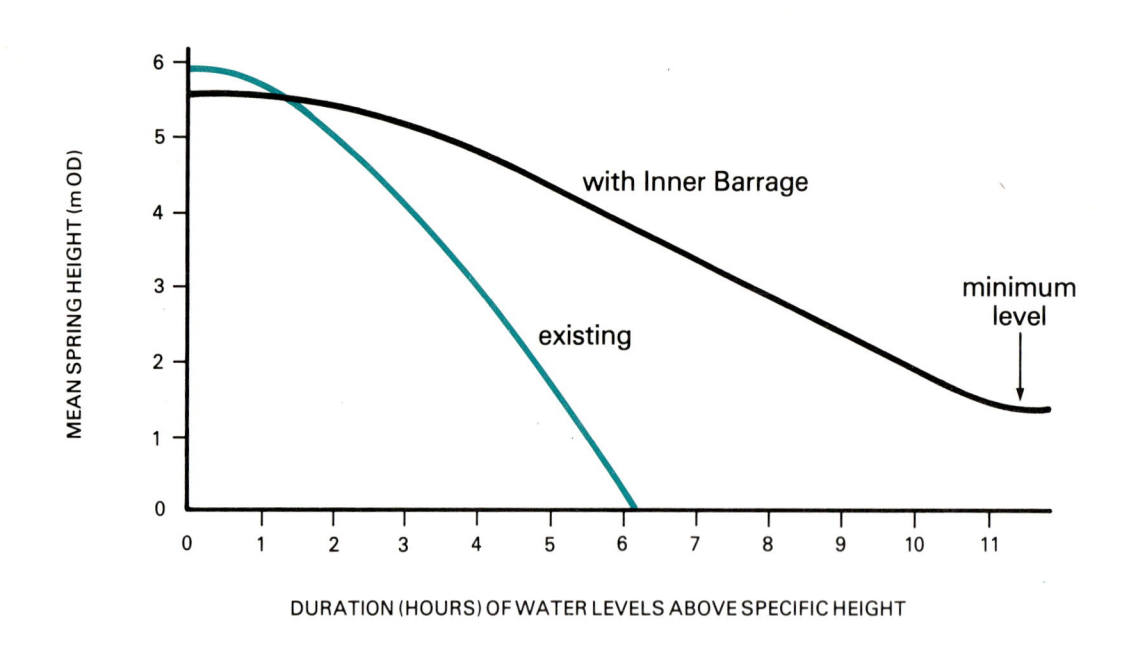

[Graph: MEAN SPRING HEIGHT (m OD) vs DURATION (HOURS) OF WATER LEVELS ABOVE SPECIFIC HEIGHT, showing "existing" curve and "with Inner Barrage" curve with "minimum level" indicated]

Fig 31 Effect of Barrage Schemes on High Water Levels

| Port | Reductions in high water levels (m) |||||||
| | Inner Barrage || Outer Barrage || Staged Scheme ||
	Spring	Neap	Spring	Neap	Spring	Neap
Swansea	0.05	0.05	0.15	0.25	0.05	0.2
Port Talbot	0.05	0.05	0.2	0.25	0.05	0.15
Barry	0.5	0.25	0.65	0.4	0.8	0.6
Cardiff	0.5	0.15	1.05	0.6	0.6	0.5
Newport	0.7	0.3	1.1	0.65	0.95	0.65
Avonmouth	0.85	0.35	1.1	0.65	1.0	0.6
Sharpness	0.85	0.5	1.1	0.6	1.0	0.6

------------ barrage location

NB Accuracy of these predictions is about ±0.2 m as discussed earlier under the heading of Water Levels

Impact on Ports and Shipping   17

General Considerations

157.   A major effect of the barrage would be to enclose some of the ports in the Severn Estuary behind a barrier. The barrage would affect ports and navigation by requiring ships to pass through locks in the barrage, by changing the water levels and, possibly, by modifying the pattern of sedimentation. The last two of these factors might also influence ports immediately outside a barrage.

158.   Bristol (Avonmouth, Portishead and Royal Portbury), Cardiff, Newport and Sharpness/Gloucester docks would be above an Inner Barrage. Barry, Bridgwater and Watchet, together with the above ports, would be above an Outer Barrage and the second basin of a Staged Scheme would enclose Bridgwater and Watchet. Neath, Port Talbot and Swansea would be outside any of these barrages.

159.   Various specific engineering recommendations related to locking and navigation requirements can now be made, as can general qualitative statements on the relative impacts of the various barrage schemes on the availability of port access, which is a key factor in the assessment of a port's economic viability.

160.   Of the vessels that presently use the Severn Estuary ports each year some 5,500 are likely to be affected by a barrage. Of these about 77% are smaller than 3000 dwt. The ports now forecast that in 1990 the number of vessels will have increased to 8,500 of which about 70% will be smaller than 3,000 dwt. However, all ports emphasise that the ability to continue to receive the present proportion of larger ships is critical to their viability since these relatively small numbers of ships carry a substantial proportion of port traffic.

Barrage Locking Requirements

161.   A simulation study of the ship movements forecast by the ports for 1990 has shown that two locks would be required in a barrage to provide security of operation and to limit delays at the barrage to less than 2 hours even if the number of vessels were to rise to 10,000 a year. Because of the higher low water levels and extended high water periods above the barrage, illustrated in Fig 30, the transit times at the port locks would be reduced sufficiently to give an overall reduction in average transit time from outside the barrage to inside the port.

162.   The currently favoured sites for locks are about 2 km off Lavernock Point for the Inner Barrage and about 4 km off Warren Point for the Outer Barrage.

163.   In order to cater for the largest vessels which can use the Estuary at present and those forecast for the future (150,000 dwt), the size of the locks would be approximately 370m long by 50m wide by 30m deep. The capital cost of a twin lock system including breakwaters would be within the range £180M to £270M.

164.   Operation and maintenance costs of the barrage locks would include staffing, operation of lock gates and tugs, maintenance dredging and additional pilotage. These would be likely to total about £5M to £6M per annum.

The Implications of Changes in Sediment Movement

165.   The port authorities are concerned about possible silting up or gross movement of navigation channels both in the main estuary and in the approaches to their docks. Sediment studies have not yet reached the point where definitive answers can be given to these questions.

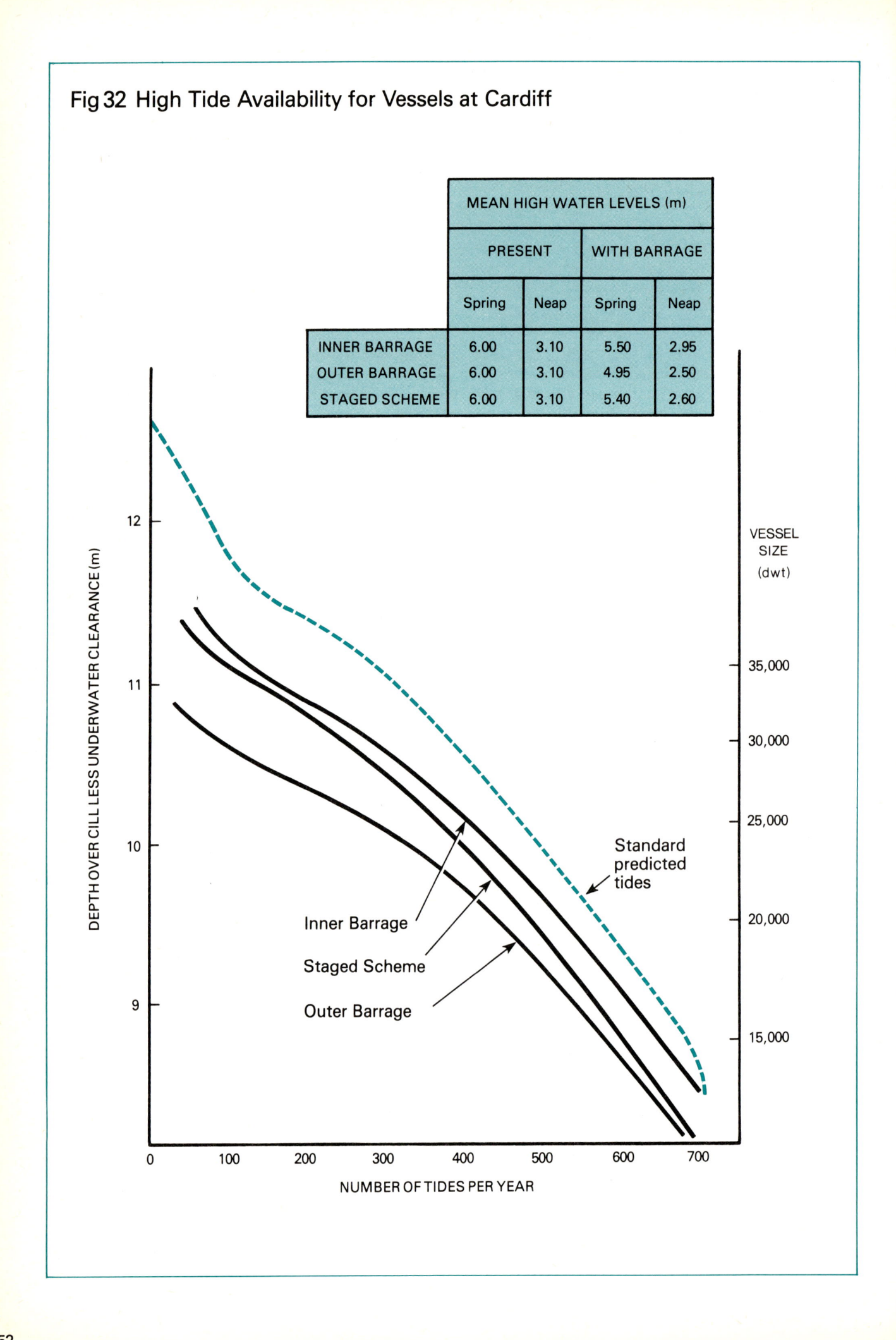

Fig 32 High Tide Availability for Vessels at Cardiff

	MEAN HIGH WATER LEVELS (m)			
	PRESENT		WITH BARRAGE	
	Spring	Neap	Spring	Neap
INNER BARRAGE	6.00	3.10	5.50	2.95
OUTER BARRAGE	6.00	3.10	4.95	2.50
STAGED SCHEME	6.00	3.10	5.40	2.60

Impact on Ports and Shipping (Continued)

166. However, numerical modelling has suggested that the average rate of sediment movement after barrage completion would be substantially reduced. Further detailed work would be required in any future study to determine whether the new, gentler tidal regime would improve navigation through reduced siltation, or whether the reduced power of the ebb currents would increase the need for dredging in navigation channels. Local effects could be important and separate modelling studies for the approaches to each port might be required.

Effect of Changed Water Levels on Shipping

167. Water levels behind the Inner Barrage would range from about present mean tide to just below present high tide, as summarised in Fig 31. The duration of the high water levels within each cycle would be extended as shown earlier. For the Inner Barrage, neap high tide levels would be typically 0.3m below present levels whereas for the Outer Barrage they would be typically 0.6m below the present levels. High water levels immediately downstream of an ebb generation barrage would be slightly reduced but the shape of the tide curve would be little changed. With the Staged Scheme, water levels inside the first stage basin would be at least as high as those resulting from an Outer Barrage, while in the second (flood generation) basin they would range from about present mid-tide to slightly below present low tide.

168. For each of the three schemes the number of tides per annum when ports are accessible to ships of a range of sizes has been calculated for the modified tidal regimes. As an example, the data for Cardiff are shown in Fig 32. No firm economic predictions can, however, be made on the basis of these data since they do not represent an absolute parameter in determining port economics. For example, they take no account of either potential disbenefits from the drop in high water levels, or potential benefits arising from the extended period of high water. It is apparent, however, that the Outer Barrage would cause the greatest concern to navigation interests and the Inner Barrage the least. Building the second flood generation stage of the Staged Scheme would cause an intermediate impact on the ports behind the first stage barrage and could close Bridgwater and Watchet to commercial shipping.

169. Generally speaking, vessels below about 15,000 dwt (50,000 for Portbury and 2,000 for Sharpness) would not be affected by any of the proposed barrage schemes. The vessels large enough to be affected represent about 12% to 25% of the numbers using the ports. For the smaller ships the post barrage retention of low water levels at Ordnance Datum or above would make locking access available at all times for 6m draft at Cardiff and Avonmouth (covering over 50% of arrivals on current sizes) and for 5m draft at Newport (about 70%).

170. With the exception of the ports within the second stage of the Staged Scheme and the possible loss to Cardiff of their largest vessels with the Outer Barrage, there are no complete exclusions of vessels at ports with any of the barrage schemes. Moreover, Cardiff has been identified as being a site at which advantage could be taken of the elimination of the present lower half of the tidal cycle to establish deep water riparian berths outside the existing impounded dock system.

171. The extent to which advantage could be taken of possible ship movement re-programming in order to avoid loss of trade is uncertain and may be outside the control of the ports. At the current level of trade, maximum use does not have to be made of all the present locking opportunities and opinions differ as to whether longer periods of availability for access on fewer occasions will be deemed to be advantageous overall. Where appointments have to be made at the present time for ship arrivals, there should be some prospect for re-programming, but the ports generally are sceptical of this approach, being apprehensive that in a climate of intense competition a reduction in the number of available tides could lose them customers.

172. For some ports, present standards of port access could be maintained by appropriate civil works at port locks or perhaps by using the barrage turbines to pump up the water level in the basin. The cost and practicability of these solutions have yet to be evaluated in detail.

Fig 33 Visual Impact of a Barrage

The visual impact of the barrage structure in the scale of the estuary will be small except when viewed from close to the barrage (see Plates 1, 2 & 4). The Inner Barrage has proposed landfalls between Sully Island and Lavernock Point on the Welsh coast and at Brean Down on the English coast. Sully Island and the coast of Lavernock Point are sites of special scientific interest, mainly on geological grounds although the former is also of interest for birds. Both have been designated as a Rural Recreation Area (for informal countryside activities) by South Glamorgan County Council. Brean Down is a nature reserve and an area of scientific and archaeological interest. Landing the barrage at the end of Brean Down, with an access tunnel running along the length of the peninsula, seems an attractive solution. This should minimise disturbance to the various sites of interest and also the visual impact.

The Outer Barrage's Welsh landfall is an Aberthaw, alongside the power station which presently dominates the Welsh coast when seen from across the estuary. This landfall is outside the limit of the South Glamorgan Heritage Coast. On the English side, Warren Point is close to Minehead. Thus the visual impact of either the Outer Barrage or the second basin of the Staged Scheme from Minehead could be similar to that of the Inner Barrage when viewed from Weston-super-Mare.

An important general point arising from the concept of a Staged Scheme is the change in the present character of the foreshore along the enclosed coastline. The second basin of a Staged Scheme, if operated in flood generation mode, would give water levels varying between about present mid-tide and low water. Moving the water line to seawards in this way would have a marked visual effect which would not occur to the same extent with a simple ebb generation scheme. The upper part of the present foreshore would change its character by becoming scrubland or perhaps agricultural land. There would be some scope for managing the character and use of this new marginal land to benefit the community. The question of whether this change is likely to be acceptable is an important issue in the overall acceptability of the Staged Scheme.

The cliffs along the Welsh and English shores, which contain various features of geological interest, would be less accessible over a greater length with an Outer Barrage than with an Inner Barrage. The second Basin of the Staged Scheme would improve access to and reduce erosion of the enclosed English shore.

The number of transmission lines leading away (in various directions) from the barrage landfalls would be about double for the Outer Barrage than for the Inner Barrage or the Staged Scheme. The visual impact of these would therefore be much greater for the Outer Barrage.

Recreation and Amenity   18

Present Situation

173. The use of the Severn Estuary for recreation is at present limited by the existing combination of high tidal range and strong currents, high water turbidity and expanses of mud exposed at low tide. Only around 2,000 boats use the estuary at present compared with Southampton Water and the Solent which are used by over 20,000 boats with facilities planned for a further 10,000.

174. There is comparatively little angling, water skiing, swimming and subaqua sport in the Severn Estuary. Angling for migratory fish in the rivers upstream of the Inner Barrage is an important recreation, with some 6,000 participants for salmon alone. Thirteen wild-fowling clubs with over 500 members use the English and Welsh shores. Bird watching takes place, particularly at Bridgwater Bay and Slimbridge, the latter having about 200,000 visitors a year.

175. The main holiday resorts are Penarth, Clevedon, Burnham-on-Sea, Barry Island, Weston-super-Mare and Minehead, the largest being Weston-super-Mare which ranks in the top ten British holiday resorts for staying visitors. Local authorities in Bristol and South Glamorgan are considering development of their older dock areas as water leisure centres.

Recreation Opportunities with a Barrage

176. The construction of a barrage across the estuary would create a large area of protected water in which the tidal range and current velocities would be much reduced. This would make the estuary much more attractive for boats of all sizes, and for other water-based recreation, including possibly sea fishing.

177. About 2 million people live around the estuary. This population together with good existing road and rail links to the Midlands and London and access to the inland waterway system should stimulate growth of leisure activities.

178. Opportunities are likely to exist, subject to planning constraints, for marina construction, sea-going hire fleets (sail and power), Sports Council-type sail training centres and a range of holiday accommodation. Boat moorings and marina berths would eventually increase from the present 1,500 to about 10,000. A five to tenfold increase in dinghies and day boats also seems likely. An increase in boating could increase the requirement for all the associated service industries in the area, such as boat building and chandlery. The barrage itself might attract up to half a million visitors a year.

179. The Committee considers that improved amenity and recreation could be a socially important benefit of a barrage. However, in financial terms the benefit might be small, amounting to only £1-3M per annum, depending on the level of additional investment in recreational facilities. Nevertheless, the social value of health and enjoyment arising from these improved facilities should not be underestimated.

180. Increased leisure use of the estuary would need careful zoning to avoid conflict both between the various recreational activities and with commercial shipping, commercial salmon fishing and environmental conservation interests.

Fig 34 Cost of a Public Road over the Barrage

Single carriageway maintenance crossing

    Box beam over sluices and caissons (including ramps)
        7700m @ £6.3M/km = £48.4M

    Single carriageway on embankment
        9700m @ £0.8M/km = £7.8M

    Low level crossing over shiplocks = £1.5M

    Total cost = £57.7M

Dual carriageway public road

    Box beam over sluices and caissons
        7300m @ £8.4M/km = £61.3M

    Dual carriageway on embankment
        10,100m @ £1.1M/km = £11.1M

    Bridge piers for ramps for high level crossing = £2.8M

    Raising embankment = £29.0M

    Acceleration/declaration lanes at bridge = £0.3M

    Low level crossing of shiplocks for maintenance access = £1.5M

    Total costs = £106.0M

Therefore, cost of uprating the maintenance road to public dual carriageway standard = £48.3M

Approximate cost of links to M4 and M5 motorways
    26km @ £1-2M/km (depending on routing) = £26-52M

Full additional cost of dual carriageway estuary crossing = £74.3-100.3M

Recreation and Amenity (Continued)

Amenity Impacts of a Barrage

181. The main impact on local amenity would be in the vicinity of the landfall sites where changes in visual aspect and land use would be inevitable, particularly arising from the need for power transmission from the barrage. Whilst the barrage would change the view from the shore, this might only be significant near the landfall sites. Since the estuary is ten kilometres or more wide at the proposed barrage sites, perspective effects would ensure that a barrage would not dominate the horizon when viewed against the opposite shore.

182. Careful design of the barrage would be needed to preserve the quality of some amenity beaches, particularly at Weston and Barry, which might otherwise suffer from deposition of fine sediment. Suitable positioning of sluices could enable this effect to be minimised but, if it occurred, maintenance would be required either by cleaning the beaches or replenishing the sand until the fine sediments stabilised.

183. Construction of a barrage would have some impact on local amenity especially at the caisson fabrication sites. Sites for these have not yet been positively identified, but the Welsh coast west of Barry should provide a suitable combination of access from land and to an adjacent deep water channel. Most of the construction material for the barrage would be brought in by sea, which would limit the impact of construction work on local amenities at landfall sites. However, transport of some material from shore to build the upper levels of the embankments is envisaged. Accommodating the various requirements for bases, stock-piling, shipping, transportation of labour and materials on land, and power transmission, would have important implications for planning of land use in the areas concerned. Also, if production of rockfill from inland quarries should prove economic this could adversely affect the local environment.

184. Construction of a barrage would lead to the loss of some sites of geological, geomorphological and biological interest which are currently used for teaching and research purposes. A barrage landfall at Brean Down would need to avoid disturbing the two archaeological sites on this headland. This could be achieved by access to the barrage being via a tunnel running along the length of the peninsula. Thus, the amenities of Brean Down and its general appearance are unlikely to be affected.

185. The Severn Tidal Bore would be much diminished or might disappear.

Opportunity for a Road Crossing

186. A barrage offers the possibility of a second road crossing of the Severn. A single carriageway road over the barrage would in any case be needed for maintenance access, including a single swing or bascule (lifting) bridge at the locks. The direct cost of upgrading this road to a dual carriageway for public access, including an elevated crossing at the locks, would be about £48M for the Inner Barrage. (This is broadly comparable to the cost of building a second Severn Bridge adjacent to the present one.) New links to existing main roads would also be required, the cost of connecting the Inner Barrage to the M4 and M5 motorways being in the region of £26-52M. The routes for these connections have not been studied but could prove difficult in places.

187. No survey has yet been carried out to assess the usefulness of a barrage crossing. On the one hand the present pattern of traffic movement suggests that only a small proportion of road traffic now crossing the Severn Estuary is travelling to or from South West England. Should the capacity of the present Severn Bridge eventually be fully used, it is possible that a second bridge higher up the estuary might serve the interests of more road users (travelling between South Wales and London or the Midlands) better than a barrage crossing lower down. On the other hand, there may be socio-economic benefits to be obtained from linking two areas of the UK which at present have relatively poor communications. These aspects would require clarification in any further study.

Other Potential Developments in the Severn Estuary

188. In the past other ideas for exploiting the Severn Estuary have been suggested, including an airport on the Welsh Grounds and various industrial and port related developments. The compatibility of a barrage with these other uses of the estuary has not been investigated and would need to be considered in any future study.

Fig 35 A Turbine Caisson Construction Yard

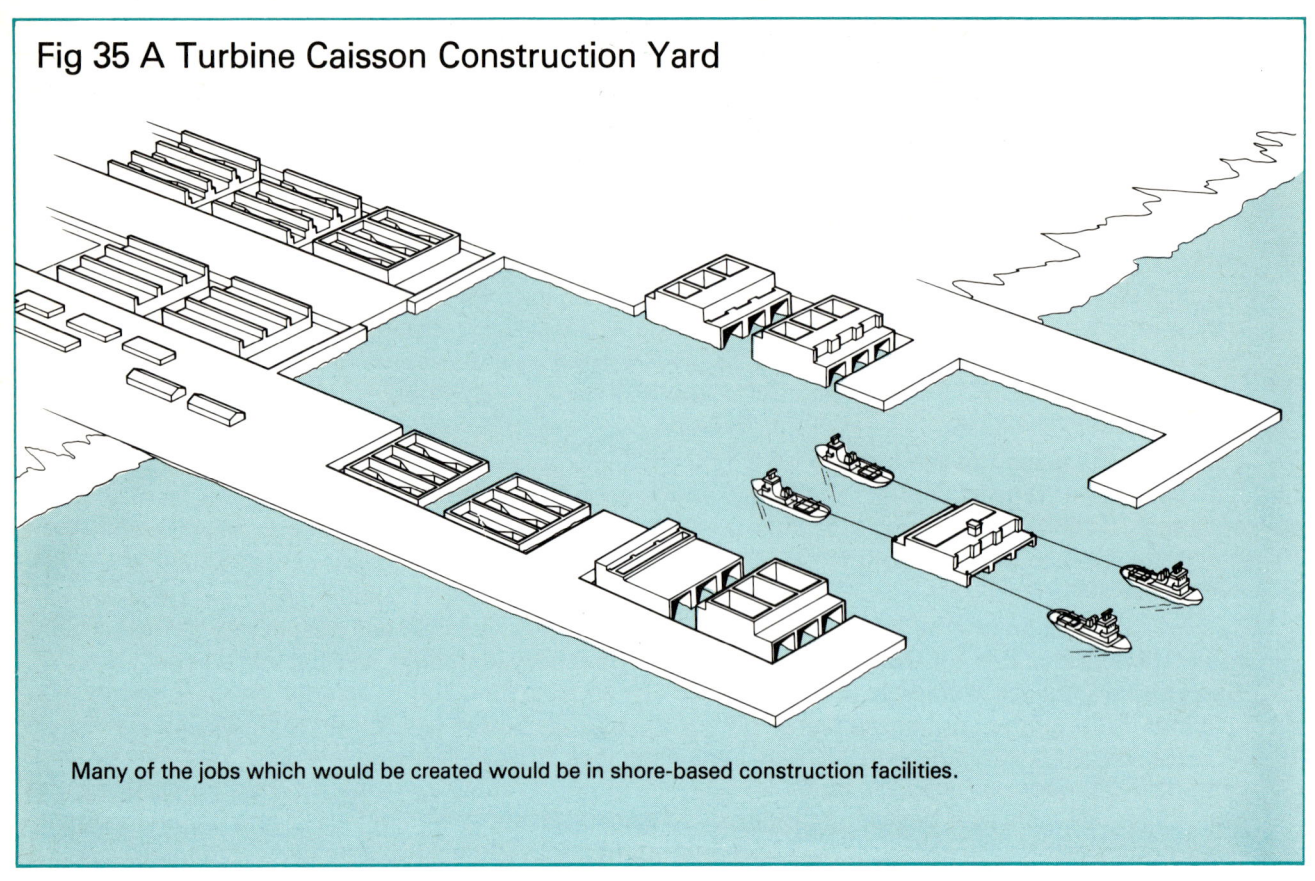

Many of the jobs which would be created would be in shore-based construction facilities.

Fig 36 Manpower Requirements During Construction of the Inner Barrage

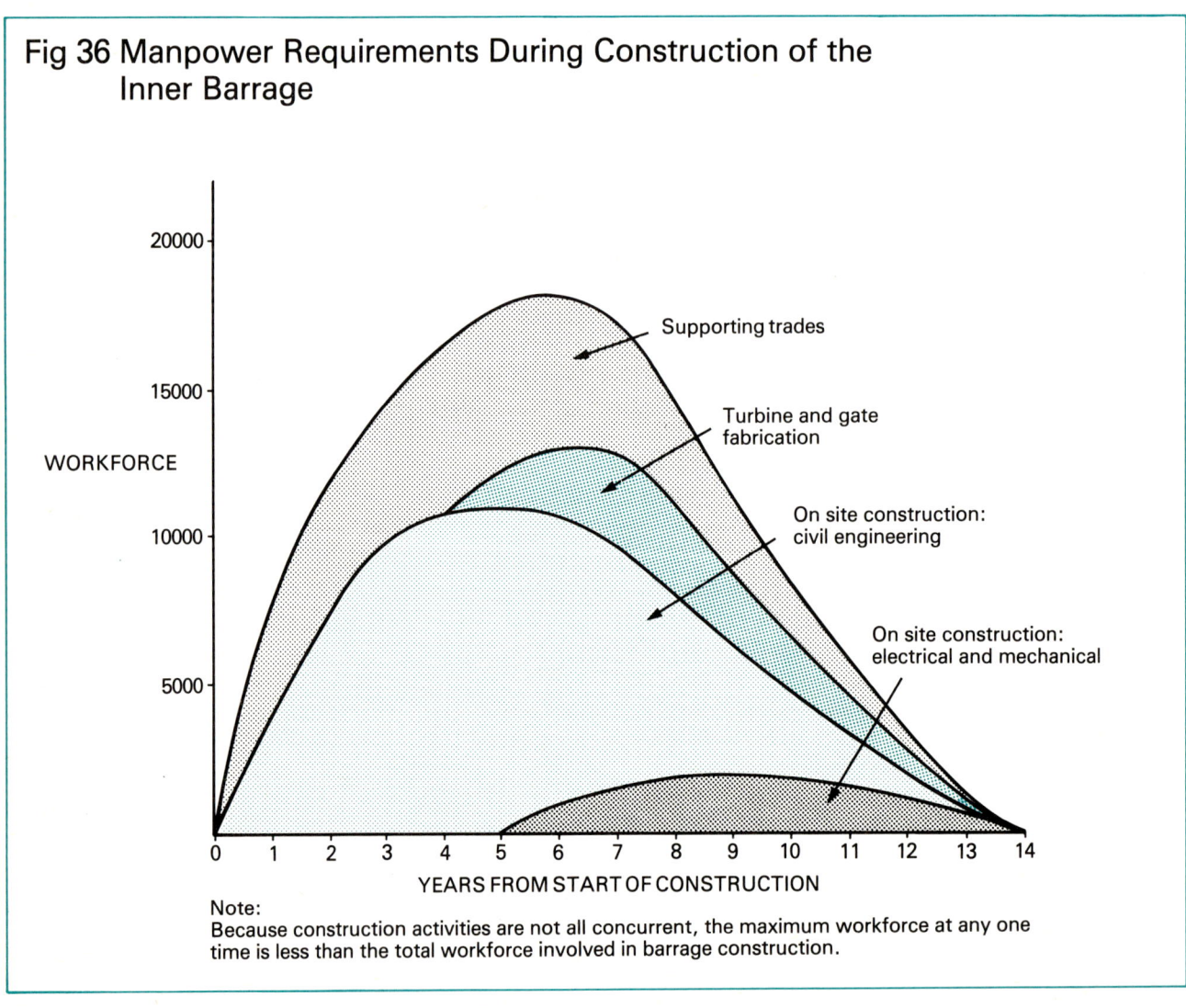

WORKFORCE

YEARS FROM START OF CONSTRUCTION

- Supporting trades
- Turbine and gate fabrication
- On site construction: civil engineering
- On site construction: electrical and mechanical

Note:
Because construction activities are not all concurrent, the maximum workforce at any one time is less than the total workforce involved in barrage construction.

Industrial Impact 19

Employment during Construction

189. A preliminary assessment of the labour requirements for the Inner Barrage suggests that a total work force of around 21,000, for various periods of up to 10 years, would be required directly for construction and supply of materials. Employment for a further 5-6,000 people could be created by the 'multiplier effect' caused by the boost to the local economy.

190. A breakdown of these numbers (Fig 36) shows that most of this employment, around 12,000 jobs, would be in mainly civil engineering activities at caisson construction yards (Fig 35), which would probably be local, and at the barrage site. A further 4,000 people would be employed in off-site fabrication of mechanical and electrical items, such as turbo-generators, electrical transmission gear and sluice gates; most of these jobs would be in other parts of the country. Around 5,000 other jobs would be created in such industries as quarrying, steel, cement, transport etc to supply materials and carry them to the barrage.

191. The total number of new jobs created in the locality of the barrage is not excessive compared with the labour force already in the area, and the various employment opportunities would be spread out in time. Thus, with some retraining, enough suitable labour would be available in South Wales and the need for labour camps and imported labour could be minimal.

Subsequent Employment

192. Operation and maintenance of the barrage might be expected to provide about 500 permanent jobs, many of which would be highly skilled.

193. Some activities, such as turbine manufacture with its skilled labour force, could provide the basis of continuing employment for manufacturing similar or related products.

Impact on Industry

194. It is uncertain whether a tidal power scheme would enhance the attractions of the region for new industrial developments. As its power output would be available through the grid, there is no obvious reason why industries should be located near to the barrage. Two potential disadvantages have been identified for both new and existing industries:

- additional controls on discharge of effluents into the basin could well be necessary as a result of constructing a barrage, and these would involve additional costs.
- raised water levels above a barrage would lead to some minor extra cost in pumping of industrial effluents.

The impact of a barrage on the ports has already been discussed separately.

Impact on Power Station Cooling

195. The generally higher water levels inside both the Inner Barrage and the Outer Barrage should improve the availability of water for cooling power stations. Oldbury and Uskmouth stations are therefore likely to benefit from a barrage. Aberthaw power station would be just inside the Outer Barrage and might however need some relatively low cost remedial works to improve dispersion of waste heat. Power station cooling outside the Inner and Outer Barrages would probably be little affected.

196. The average depth of water available for cooling at Hinkley Point would be significantly reduced if the Staged Scheme were to be constructed with its second basin operating in flood-generation mode. However, the new low water levels would not be any lower than at present. Current patterns would also be changed and it would be essential to study their impact on dispersion and recirculation of cooling water. Possible changes in patterns of sedimentation would also need to be investigated for this site. Cooling towers might have to be considered for any new development at Hinkley Point.

Fig 37 Low Lying Areas in the Severn Estuary

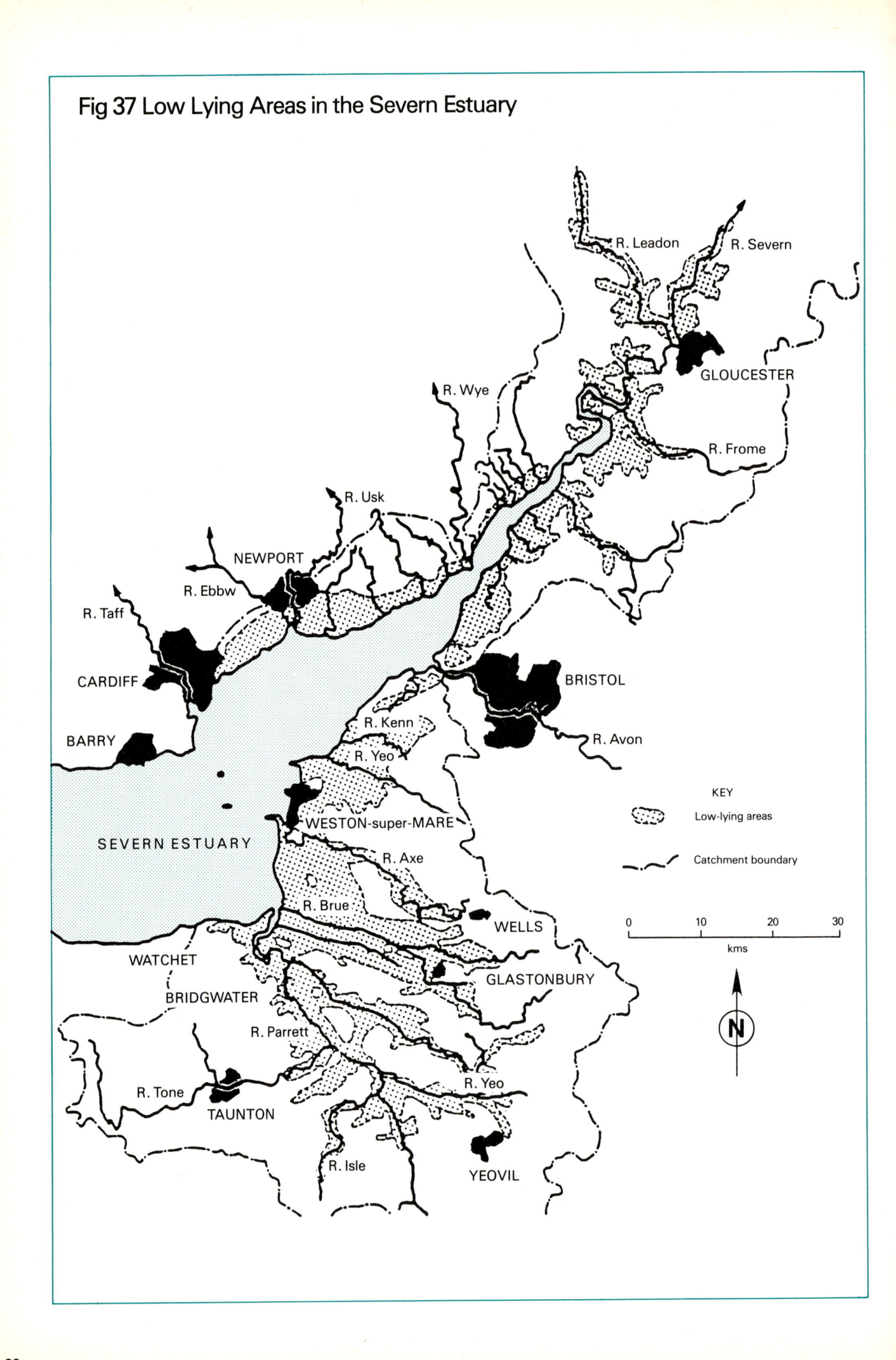

Impact on Sea Defence, Land Drainage and Agriculture   20

Sea Defence

197. The existing sea defences have much reduced the frequency of sea-water flooding of land around the Severn Estuary. These sea defence banks extend along open coasts and up sub-estuaries and channels to join with river flood banks.

198. The sea defences above the barrage would not need to be raised, because high tide levels would be lower and extreme high tides and surge tides would be kept out by the main barrage. However, these defences could in places be more susceptible to wave attack than at present because the modified tidal levels would result in wave attack occurring over a more limited range of elevations. Hence, some sections of embankment would be under wave attack for longer than at present, although the waves might be smaller because of reduced maximum water depths. In some places, there may be a need to extend or improve the surface protection of defence banks. Foundations of some defence banks and footings of some surface protection works would become permanently submerged making maintenance both more difficult and more costly.

199. However, the cost of extending the surface protection of defence banks would be relatively small (up to £10M).

Flood Protection

200. Both the Inner and Outer Barrages would, by lowering tidal high water levels, considerably reduce the risk of salt water flooding over banks within the upstream basins. It would also reduce the risk of freshwater flooding around Gloucester.

201. If either the Staged Scheme or the Outer Barrage were to be built, the risks of flooding around Bridgwater Bay and in the lower reaches of the Parrett would be diminished because of reduced high water levels. This is especially so with the Staged Scheme having its second basin operated in flood generation mode. However, in this case a weir across the Parrett might be needed to maintain depths for amenity and inland navigation.

Land Drainage

202. Land drainage is aimed at controlling soil water to the optimum required for agriculture and also as protection from flooding. The low-lying flat areas around the Severn (Fig 37) include the Somerset Levels, the Wentlooge and Caldicot Levels near Newport and areas along the Severn as far upstream as Gloucester and beyond. There are smaller areas of lowland beside the lower reaches of the Usk, Wye and Bristol Avon. In all there are some 80,000 ha of low-lying land near the estuary which is served by land drainage schemes, about half of which drains into the estuary seaward of the Holm Islands. The rivers and main drains crossing this low-lying land are embanked.

203. The main drains and rivers all drain by gravity. Most of the 70 drains up-estuary of Avonmouth discharge through outfalls at about +5m O.D. or higher. Of the 12 with bed levels lower than this, 5 are below +2.5m O.D. Some of the main drains are fitted with barriers which exclude the tides and the sediments which they carry. Land drainage into the main channels is assisted by pumping and in some cases is wholly dependent upon it.

Fig 38 Cross Section of the Somerset Levels from Burnham to Glastonbury Showing Inland Areas Below High Water Level

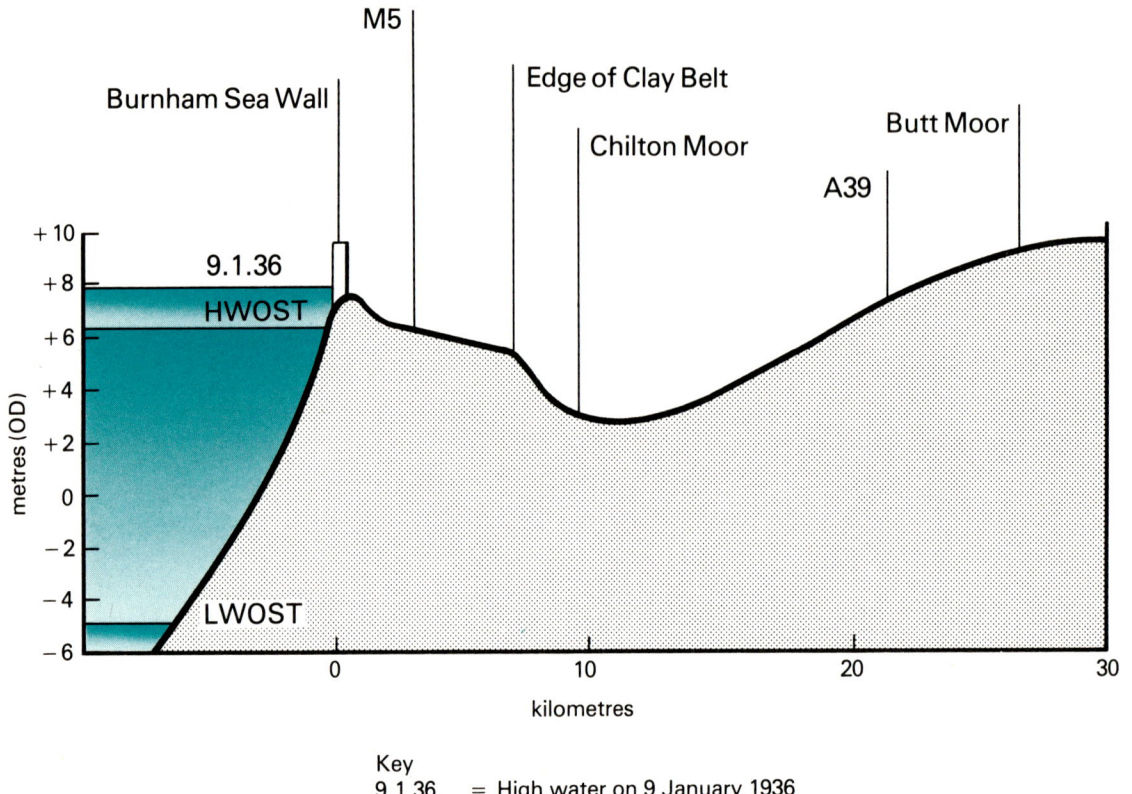

Key
9.1.36 = High water on 9 January 1936
HWOST = High water ordinary spring tide
LWOST = Low water ordinary spring tide

A flood generation barrage encircling Bridgwater Bay would benefit land drainage by lowering water levels to between present mid tide and low water. (Existing high and low water at spring tides are shown.)

Reproduced from "An Environmental Appraisal of Tidal Power Stations", Pitman, 1980, by courtesy of Dr. T. L. Shaw.

Impact on Sea Defence, Land Drainage and Agriculture (Continued)

204. The changes in water levels due to an ebb generation barrage would affect drainage around the estuary. The duration when discharge can occur would be reduced for channels with bed levels of up to +5m and substantial pumping would be required for those drains with bed levels of +2.5m or below. However, most drains would be unaffected. For all the preferred schemes suitable engineering works could be built where necessary. The Outer Barrage would require modification to the drainage of a greater land area. The nature of these works would depend both on the tidal power scheme chosen and the way in which it is operated. The most important elements are likely to be new pumping stations and outfalls and, where possible, additional storage of water at outfalls. The total capital cost would, however, be small at around £14-19M. In addition, some increased maintenance dredging of tributary river channels, to deal with possible increases in siltation, might be required, although this is very uncertain.

205. The second phase (flood generation) of the Staged Scheme would enclose Bridgwater Bay and confine tidal levels to the lower half of the present tidal range. This would improve existing land drainage in the area by increasing its efficiency, particularly near the river mouths.

Agriculture

206. There would be a small potential agricultural benefit if land drainage were to be improved by the additional works which would be needed following construction of a barrage. This would enable the water table to be maintained at a level appropriate to the soil type and crop being grown, and could enable the grazing season to be extended. However, more efficient land drainage would result in loss of wetland areas which are an important nature conservation interest. Indeed, there would be a positive nature conservation benefit in not improving drainage. Thus a balance would need to be found between the conflicting needs of nature conservation and agriculture. Protective measures might be required to conserve wetland areas of biological importance.

207. In areas where the increased minimum water levels in the estuary require greater reliance on pumped drainage of adjacent low-lying land, well-known measures might be required to prevent saline intrusion. However, the cost would be negligible at under £1M.

208. The second phase of the Staged Scheme provides more scope for land improvement, though the conflicting needs of agriculture and nature conservation would require careful consideration. This scheme would also expose a broad zone of foreshore above the new high water level to form dry land; this would affect both farming and the important Bridgwater Bay National Nature Reserve.

Fig 39 Predicted Effect of a Barrage on Cadmium Concentration

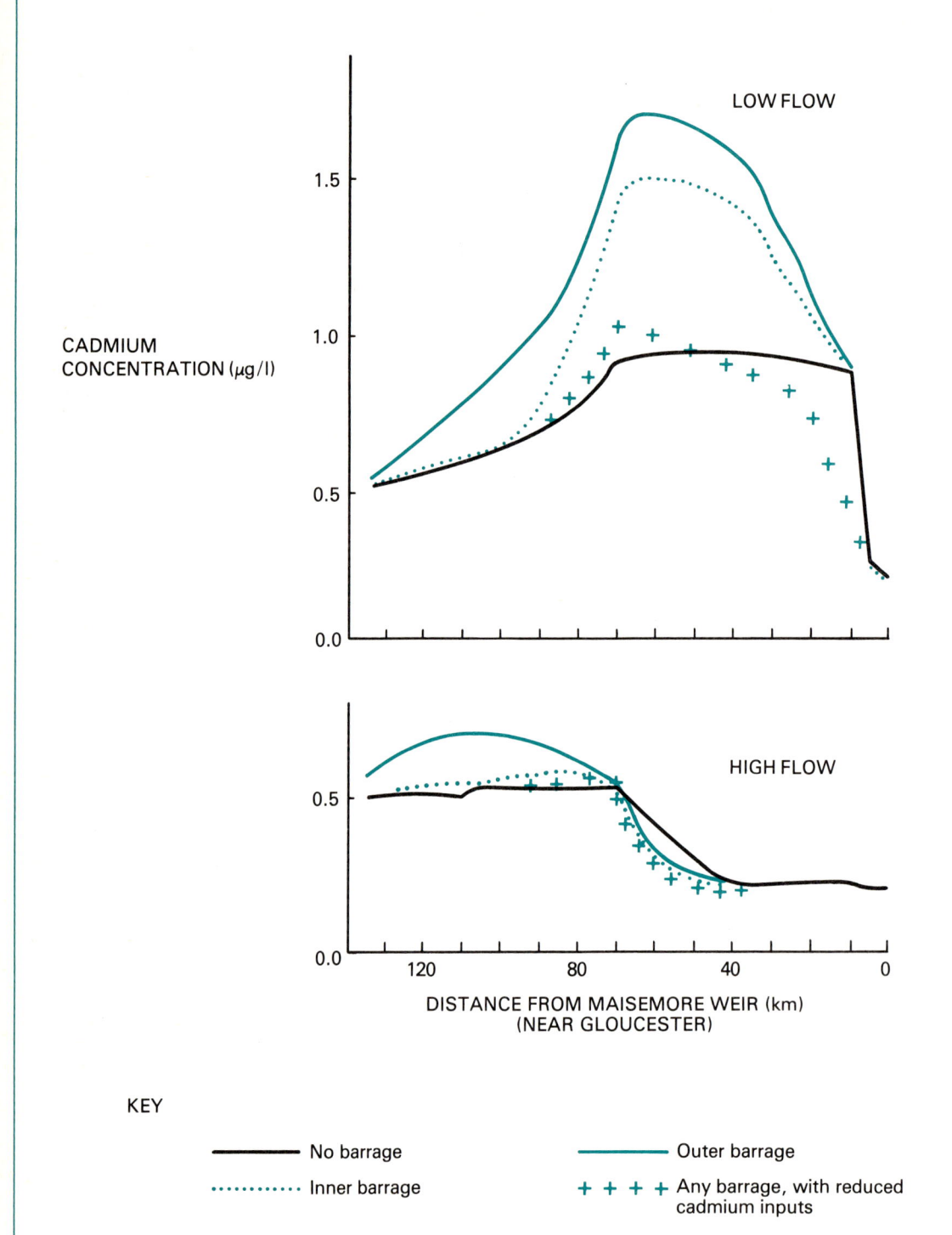

CADMIUM CONCENTRATION (µg/l)

LOW FLOW

HIGH FLOW

DISTANCE FROM MAISEMORE WEIR (km)
(NEAR GLOUCESTER)

KEY

—— No barrage
·········· Inner barrage
—— Outer barrage
+ + + + Any barrage, with reduced cadmium inputs

The figures show average cadmium distributions in the estuary at extreme river flow rates. For any of the leading barrage schemes cadmium concentrations are expected to remain well within limits currently set by the European Standard for Drinking Water (10µg/l) and the EEC Directive on Water Quality for Human Consumption (5µg/l). There are at present no standards for tidal waters but these are under consideration. It should be technically possible to undertake remedial action to avoid exceeding existing cadmium levels, if this should be required.

Impact on Water Quality

209. The suitability of an estuary for recreation, as a habitat for aquatic organisms, and for other beneficial uses is dependent on its water quality. Potential changes in water quality and their expected influences on aquatic organisms have been assessed using numerical models.

Main Estuary — Present Condition

210. The main estuary receives pollutants from many sources (including discharges of domestic and industrial waste waters, urban surface water, land drainage, sludge dumping and atmospheric deposition) but relative to its large size the polluting loads are small. The degree of contamination is thus low except close to outfalls. In the estuary generally there are only small elevations above the natural background concentrations of oxygen-demanding constituents such as Biochemical Oxygen Demand (BOD) and ammonia; of readily assimilable algal nutrients, such as total inorganic nitrogen and dissolved orthophosphate; and of heavy metals including cadmium and nickel. The contents of heavy metals in some aquatic animals are above those typically found in animals living in unpolluted habitats. However, these animals are not sold for human consumption.

211. The oxygen demanding constituents and dissolved orthophosphate are derived principally from discharges of sewage and sewage effluents. Land drainage into rivers contributes the major part of total inorganic nitrogen. Discharges of industrial waste water and atmospheric deposition are principal sources of heavy metals.

212. The water is turbid landward of the Holm Islands, owing to continual resuspension of bottom deposits by the tides. Much of the incident light is absorbed and hence the rate of growth of algae is restricted. This in turn restricts the productivity of organisms which feed on algae and of predators in the acquatic ecosystem.

Main Estuary — Predictions

213. In addition to increasing the average water depth in the basin and hence the degree of dilution of pollutants, an ebb generation barrage would reduce rates of longitudinal dispersion and the efficiency of absorption of oxygen from the air. Predictions of water characteristics have been made for various assumed reductions in rates of dispersion. Present conclusions are based on a 75% reduction in rates of dispersion and a 50% reduction in oxygen transfer efficiency. These reductions are the maximum considered likely.

214. These maximum changes would move the freshwater/saltwater interface to seaward by between 5 and 30 km depending on river flow. At worst there would be a doubling of the concentrations of "conservative" pollutants, such as cadmium and nickel, which behave approximately as if influenced only by dilution and dispersion (Fig 39). Concentrations of non-conservative constituents behind the barrage, including BOD, ammonia, coliform bacteria, total inorganic nitrogen and dissolved orthophosphate, and also of dissolved oxygen, would, however, be little changed (Fig 40).

215. Turbidity would be reduced because of the generally lower currents. More light would penetrate and thus the rate of growth of algae in some parts of the estuary would increase, particularly in the first year or two after introduction of a barrage. Although algal populations might occasionally reach nuisance levels in places at first, increased growth of their predators would probably eventually cause the numbers of algae to decrease nearly to pre-barrage levels.

Fig 40 Predicted Effect of a Barrage on E.Coli Concentration

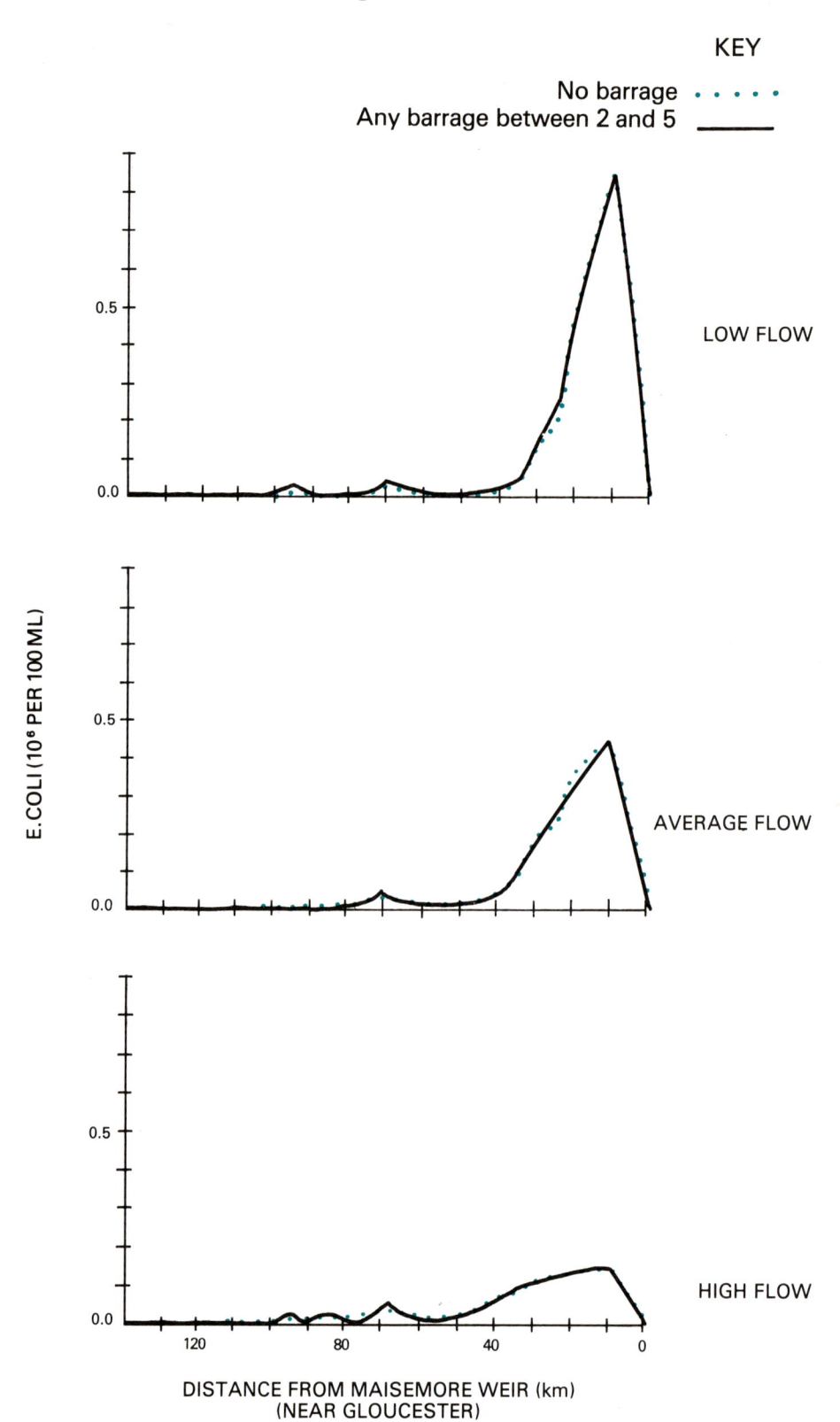

KEY
No barrage · · · · ·
Any barrage between 2 and 5 ──────

LOW FLOW

E.COLI (10^6 PER 100 ML)

AVERAGE FLOW

HIGH FLOW

DISTANCE FROM MAISEMORE WEIR (km)
(NEAR GLOUCESTER)

The figures show concentrations of *E. Coli* bacteria under different river flow conditions. Construction of a barrage anywhere between lines 2 and 5 is predicted to have negligible effect. Similar very small differences between conditions with and without a barrage are found for dissolved oxygen, orthophosphate, ammonia, inorganic nitrogen and BOD, but the shapes of the curves for some substances, such as dissolved oxygen, are different.

Impact on Water Quality (Continued)

216. Numbers of bacteria at the shore near sewage outfalls would be little changed. Slight increases in temperature would probably occur near the outfalls of open channels from which power station cooling waters are discharged. Water quality to seaward of a barrage would be little affected.

Sub-Estuaries — Present Conditions

217. Of the seven most important sub-estuaries, the Rhymney, Ely and Wye are only lightly polluted. The Taff is moderately polluted and the Avon, Parrett and Usk more severely contaminated, particularly by oxygen-demanding substances. Concentrations of dissolved oxygen are appreciably below the air-saturation value in the central reaches of these last three sub-estuaries and in the Usk are at times low enough to prejudice passage of migratory fish. Reductions are greatest during conditions of low flow and spring tides. The association of worst conditions with spring tides is probably due to the relatively high content of oxygen-demanding mud that they bring into suspension.

Sub-Estuaries — Predictions

218. A barrage would reduce tidal movement in sub-estuaries so that water would be less saline generally. At low water, however, reaches near the mouths of sub-estuaries would be more saline. Turbidity would be much reduced at all times. Dissolved oxygen content at low water, which is the critical time, would probably be reduced in the middle reaches. However, the extent of any change in dissolved oxygen content is dependent, both under existing conditions and with a barrage, on the oxygen demand of mud which cannot accurately be predicted. Depletion of dissolved oxygen is likely to be important only in the more polluted estuaries.

Costs

219. It is not yet clear to what extent any adverse changes in water quality would require remedial action, assuming such changes did not contravene nationally accepted standards or EEC regulations. This would require a policy decision. If, however, it should prove necessary to maintain water quality as far as practicable at the present standard in the main and sub-estuaries, this could be achieved by reducing pollution loads, probably by not more than 50%. The likely total capital cost of controlling all pollutants similarly by introduction of new treatment works would be between £120M and £230M. Running costs of these works might amount to £12-24M per annum.

220. Changes in salinity would be inevitable with any cross-estuary barrage and their elimination would be impracticable.

Fig 41 Nature Conservation in the Severn Area

NATURE CONSERVATION PRACTICE

One of the principal themes of British nature conservation practice is the identification and safeguarding of a series of areas where the most important elements of our wildlife and natural features occur. In 1977, A Nature Conservation Review (NCR) was published by NCC and NERC which describes a national series of key biological sites that should be safeguarded as a basis of the total range of variation in natural and semi-natural ecosystems in Britain. These key sites are of equivalent nature conservation value to National Nature Reserves (NNR) and many are so designated. The evaluation and designation of key sites is a continuing process.

SITES OF BIOLOGICAL IMPORTANCE

Bridgwater Bay, the New Grounds at Slimbridge and the Severn Estuary between its head and a line from Cardiff to Weston-super-Mare are designated 'key sites' in the review, predominantly as habitats for wading birds and wildfowl. Bridgwater Bay is also a statutory National Nature Reserve and a designated site under the Ramsar Convention. In addition two coastal sites, Berrow Marsh and Brean Down/Uphill Cliff, are included on account of their important plant communities. Two fresh water key sites that would be affected by a barrage are the River Wye and Shapwick Heath NNR and adjacent areas in the Somerset Levels.

SITES OF GEOLOGICAL INTEREST

There are also a number of sites of geological and geomorphological importance in the area, many of which are considered of national importance and will be included in the Geological Conservation Review (GCR) which NCC is currently preparing. At least one of these sites, the Lilstock — Blue Anchor exposure, is of international importance, being the standard for the base of the Hettangian stage of the Lower Jurassic.

SITES OF SPECIAL SCIENTIFIC INTEREST

NCC has the statutory duty to notify Sites of Special Scientific Interest (SSSIs) to relevant authorities. These are areas of particular interest because of their nature conservation value and include NCR and GCR key sites. The figure overleaf shows the position of SSSIs along the estuary, including wetland sites in the Gwent Levels and upstream of Gloucester. The river Usk is now reckoned as equivalent in value to parts of the Wye and may be notified shortly as a SSSI. Both rivers have important ecosystems with migratory salmon and shad.

NON-STATUTORY RESERVES

The Severn Estuary area also includes a number of non-statutory nature reserves such as the Wildfowl Trust's Refuge at Slimbridge, the Peterstone Wildfowl Refuge, Lavernock Point, which belong to local trusts, the National Trust's coastal properties of Middle Hope and Redcliffe Bay, and the islands of Steep Holm and Flat Holm administered respectively by the Kenneth Allsop Memorial Trust and the South Glamorgan County Council. Magor Marsh in the Gwent Levels is managed as a nature reserve by the Gwent Trust for Nature Conservation. Many of these non-statutory reserves also have SSSI status.

Impact on the Ecosystem and Nature Conservation   22

Importance of the Severn Estuary Area

221. The Severn Estuary is a complex mosaic of inter-dependent biological, geological and geomorphological elements. Parts of the estuary have been judged to be of both national and international biological importance and appropriate nature conservation designations have been applied to substantial areas (see Figs 41 and 42).

222. The extreme tidal range in the Severn results in the exposure of a large intertidal area. There are extensive mudflats colonised by invertebrates which provide food for large numbers of wading birds and wildfowl, particularly shelduck. The tops of these flats are stabilised by salt tolerant plants which form a ribbon of saltmarshes along the estuary. These are important as an integral part of the total ecosystem and in providing a roosting and breeding area for birds.

223. In the upper reaches of the estuary and behind the stretches of soft shore are extensive wetlands. Some of these represent a significant proportion of this habitat in Britain with their unique association of plants and invertebrates. Such areas are also important for birds which feed there over winter or on passage. The Somerset Levels provide an important habitat for otters.

224. The rivers Usk and Wye have important riverine ecosystems and, together with the Severn, are nationally important salmon rivers.

Sites of International Importance

225. The whole of the Severn Estuary qualifies as a site of international importance as a wintering ground for five species of wading birds (dunlin, grey plover, ringed plover, curlew and redshank) and shelduck. The Welsh and Middle Grounds are also important in their own right for dunlin and grey plover. Near the head of the estuary the New Grounds at Slimbridge are important as a winter haunt of wildfowl, especially the European white-fronted goose and the Bewick Swan. Bridgwater Bay is an important site for the dunlin and notable for wildfowl, being of particular interest as the more important of the two known British moulting grounds for shelduck.

226. The international significance of Bridgwater Bay is recognised by the UK Government in their ratification of the Ramsar Convention. Obligations accepted by the UK Government under this agreement include compensating so far as possible for any loss or diminution of a wetland site that may become necessary in the urgent national interest, in particular by creating additional compensatory nature reserves for water fowl and by protecting, either in the same ground or elsewhere, an adequate part of the original habitat. The New Grounds at Slimbridge has been proposed as an addition to the list of British 'Ramsar' Sites.

227. The EEC bird directive calls for member states to pay particular attention to the protection of wetlands, particularly those of international importance.

Impacts on the Natural Environment

228. Any barrage scheme would cause some alterations to the natural environment. However, the full extent of the likely physical changes are at present unknown and hence it is not possible to predict accurately the consequences for the habitats, together with the animals and plants they support, and the earth science interest. Nevertheless, it is possible to make some tentative predictions.

Fig 42 Sites of Nature Conservation Importance in the Severn Estuary Area

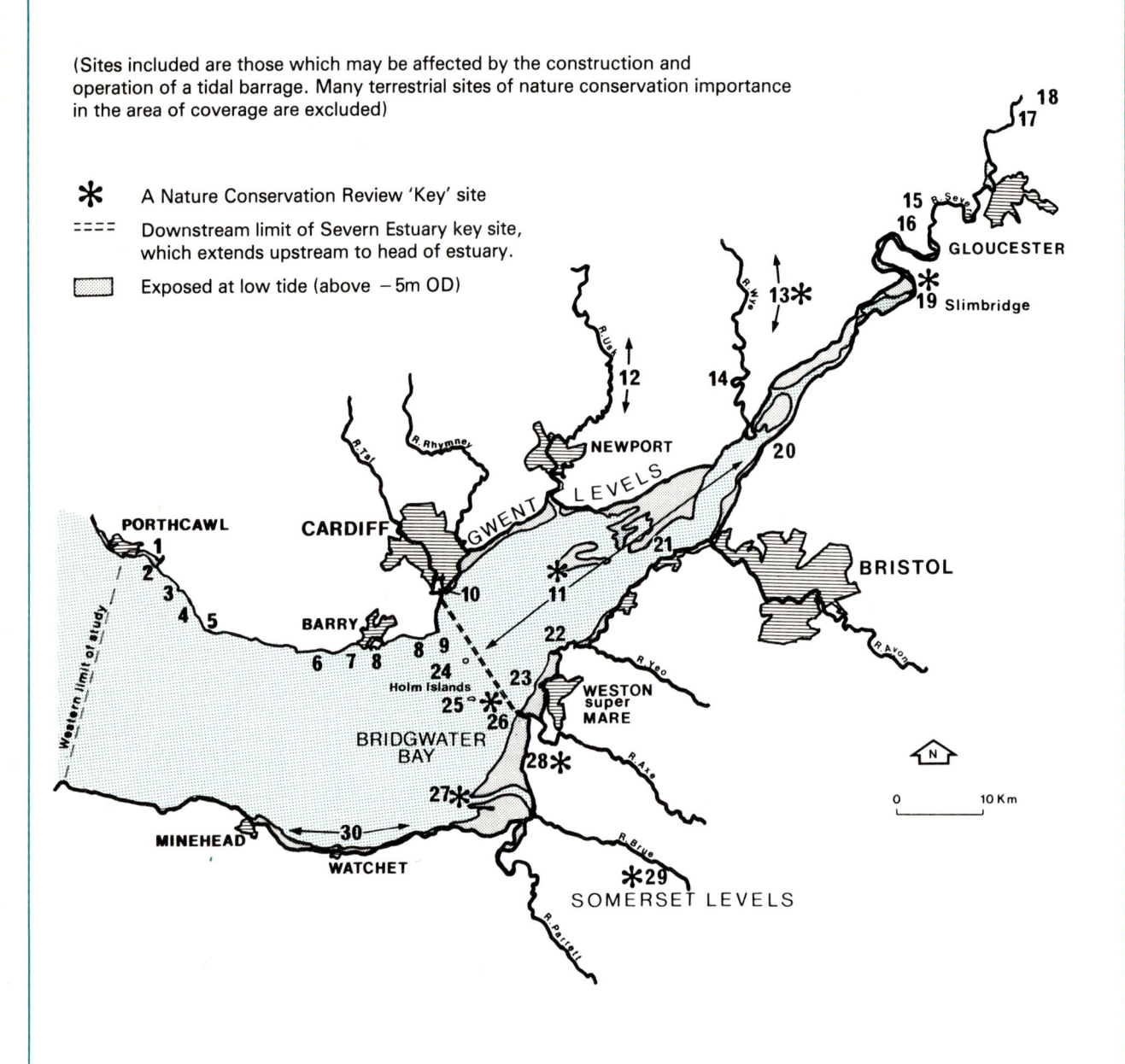

(Sites included are those which may be affected by the construction and operation of a tidal barrage. Many terrestrial sites of nature conservation importance in the area of coverage are excluded)

✳ A Nature Conservation Review 'Key' site

==== Downstream limit of Severn Estuary key site, which extends upstream to head of estuary.

▒ Exposed at low tide (above −5m OD)

KEY TO SITES

1 MERTHYR MAWR: dune system and fossil cliffline; biological interest
2 SUTTON FLATS: Triassic? conglomerate
3 SOUTHERNDOWN COAST: Lower Jurassic site; botanical interest
4 MONKNASH COAST:
5 NASH LIGHTHOUSE MEADOW:
6 EAST ABERTHAW COAST: ⎤ botanical interest
7 PORTHKERRY CLIFFS: ⎦
8 LITTLE ISLAND — NELL'S POINT AND SULLY ISLAND: angular unconformity
9 PENARTH COAST: Lower Jurassic site; botanical interest
10 TAF/ELY ESTUARY: wader feeding ground
11 SEVERN ESTUARY: wintering wader populations on intertidal flats
12 RIVER USK: ⎤ riverine flora and fauna
13 RIVER WYE: ⎦
14 WYE GORGE: incised meanders; limestone woodland to saltmarsh
15 WALMORE COMMON: freshwater wetland
16 GARDEN CLIFF: ⎤ Rhaetic sites
17 WAINLODE CLIFF: ⎦
18 GLOUCESTER — TEWKESBURY: river and floodplain for wintering wildfowl and/or of botanical interest
19 NEW GROUNDS, SLIMBRIDGE: saltmarsh; wintering wildfowl
20 AUST CLIFF: Rhaetic site with fossil vertebrate fauna
21 PORTISHEAD — BLACK NORE COAST: Palaeozoic/Mesozoic stratigraphy
22 MIDDLE HOPE: ⎤ Lower Carboniferous volcanic sites
23 SPRING COVE: ⎦
24 FLAT HOLM: ⎤ Island ecosystems
25 STEEP HOLM: ⎦
26 BREAN DOWN: Limestone vegetation; Pleistocene deposits with fossil mammalian fauna
27 BRIDGWATER BAY NATIONAL NATURE RESERVE and 'RAMSAR' SITE: Important waterfowl habitat ratified by international convention; shingle complexes
28 BERROW MARSH & DUNES: botanical and physiographic interest
29 SHAPWICK HEATH NATIONAL NATURE RESERVE: raised mire, marsh and fen
30 BLUE ANCHOR — LILSTOCK COAST: Lower Jurassic site

Impact on the Ecosystem and Nature Conservation (Continued)

229. Although construction of a barrage would result in the elimination or reduction of areas of interest, some new habitats would be created, as has been the Dutch experience with their Delta project. While some of these new habitats might provide alternative areas for sites lost, e.g. new intertidal mudflats, others could potentially contribute new habitats not at present well represented in the Severn Estuary area, e.g. reed beds.

Impact on Birds

230. The intertidal flats of most British and European estuaries have been continually reduced over the years and, if they already carry a full capacity of birds in winter, any loss of feeding grounds in the Severn could result in an overall reduction of certain species. However, the question of whether or not our estuaries contain unused food resources available to birds is still a matter of debate. The shelduck is perhaps the species which might be most critically affected by a barrage.

Wading Birds and Shelduck

231. Wading birds and shelduck feed on invertebrates which inhabit the intertidal mudbanks of the estuary. Construction of a barrage would:

- reduce tidal ranges and hence the intertidal areas available for feeding
- cause changes in the shape of the tidal curve, reducing the time available for feeding
- lower salinity in the upper estuary behind the barrage and hence reduce the density of those particular invertebrates suitable for wading birds (but not shelduck) feeding on some of the remaining banks
- produce a more sheltered regime causing an extension of the saltmarsh grass *Spartina,* further reducing the area of intertidal mud.

232. On the basis of these four disadvantages a reduction in the number of wading birds and shelduck supported by the estuary would be expected. However, the relationship between these birds and their invertebrate foods is still imperfectly understood and other changes could be to their advantage. For example, the reduced tidal velocity over the remaining intertidal flats means that the surface would become less mobile, encouraging a higher population density of the organisms on which they feed. Also, many waders feed at the water edge and the extent of this feeding zone would be little changed by the presence of a barrage, although its food content could be depleted more rapidly.

233. Freedom from disturbance is almost certainly one of the key factors in allowing shelduck to moult in Bridgwater Bay and significant increase in activity in this area could be detrimental. In addition, any reduction in the density or availability of food for birds during their flightless period could be critical.

234. Since the water levels in Bridgwater Bay would be little affected by the Inner Barrage, this scheme could have much less impact on wading birds and shelduck in this area than either the Outer Barrage or the Staged Scheme.

Fig 43 Shore Birds Over-wintering in the Severn Estuary

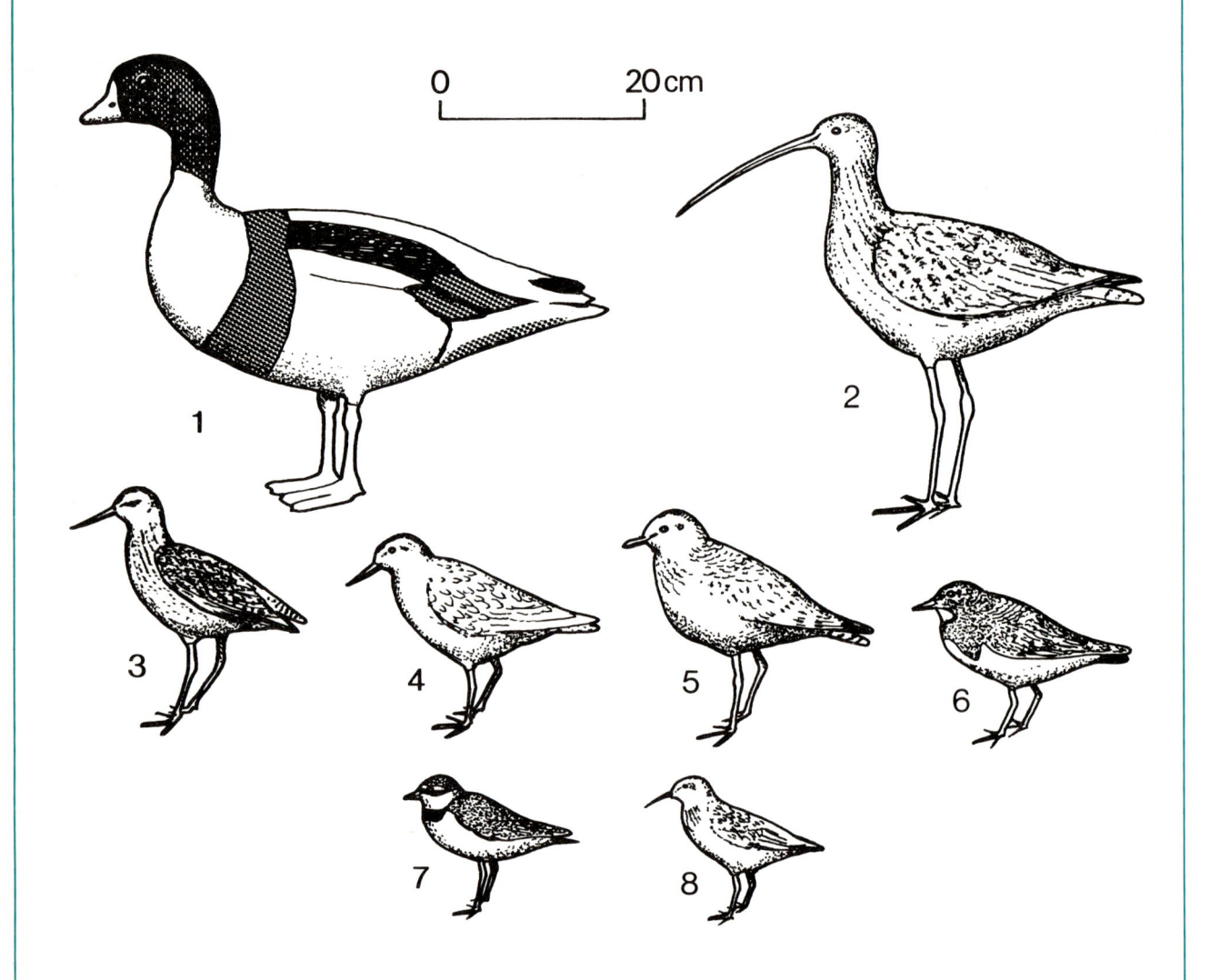

Common over-wintering species in the Severn Estuary:
1. Shelduck *(Tadorna tadorna)*; 2. Curlew *(Numenius arquata);* 3. Redshank *(Tringa totanus);* 4. Knot *(Calidris canutus);* 5. Grey plover *(Pluvialis squatarola);* 6. Turnstone *(Arenaria interpres);* 7. Ringed plover *(Charadrius hiaticula);* 8. Dunlin *(Calidris alpina)*

Illustration reproduced from John and Ann Edington's book "Ecology and Environmental Planning" by courtesy of the authors and publishers Chapman and Hall.

Impact on the Ecosystem and Nature Conservation (Continued)

Other Birds

235. Other species of birds might benefit from the construction of a barrage and indeed some new species, e.g. reed bed warblers, could be attracted to the area. Ecosystem modelling studies show that the total numbers of invertebrates, both bottom feeding and especially suspension feeding organisms, could increase markedly above the barrage. Consideration of the relevant food chains suggests that the large increase in suspension feeders might for example lead to increased populations of those birds which feed on shellfish, e.g. seaducks. However, increases in the numbers and variety of other bird species might not be regarded by some nature conservation organisations as compensation for any losses of wading birds and shelduck which might occur.

236. Although the construction of any barrage could alter the conditions for wildfowl in the upper estuary (e.g. Slimbridge) through the lowering of high water levels, this might not be a disadvantage since the geese and wigeon which over-winter in this region (Slimbridge) prefer to feed on the water meadows which would be relatively unaffected. The main threat in this region could be from increased recreational development which the barrage might encourage.

Migratory Fish

237. Salmon, sea trout, shad, lamprey and eels are known to migrate through the Severn Estuary. All these except the eels are born in rivers, migrate to sea for most of their adult lives, and return to spawn. Eels are believed to spawn in the Sargasso Sea and migrate through the estuary as elvers. They live in the rivers for several years before migrating back to sea to spawn.

238. In this study work has been concentrated on the two most important commercial species, namely salmon and eel. The salmon fisheries, particularly of the Wye, are of national importance, being 35% of the England and Wales rod catch. Considering the total revenue generated by salmon angling and commercial fishing, salmon fisheries in the rivers entering the Severn Estuary are valued at about £6M annually. Eel fishing has some local importance, the elver catch in the Severn being worth around £0.4M annually. In a nature conservation context, shad and lamprey are significant.

239. To obtain a full picture of the effect of a barrage on salmon, and on eels which should be no more affected than salmon, would require several year's work. However, it is possible to make a number of preliminary comments:

- the incoming fish are likely to pass through the main barrage without problems since on the flood tide the sluices would all be open. However, small fish such as eels may be drawn back through the turbines on the ebb tide and may thus make more than one passage through the barrage.

- it is not yet known if adult salmon could pass unharmed into a flood generating basin (Stage 2 scheme). To reach their natal rivers migratory fish would have to locate the exit sluices and successfully negotiate the Inner Barrage. However, although some migratory fish could be trapped in the basin, the known behaviour of the salmon would suggest that the majority would eventually escape and be attracted upstream towards their "home" river.

- almost all outward migrating smolts should be able to pass through the turbines without long-term damage. North American experiments on run-of-river schemes suggest high survival rates in conditions which are more severe than would occur in a Severn Barrage.

Fig 44 Life Cycle of the Salmon

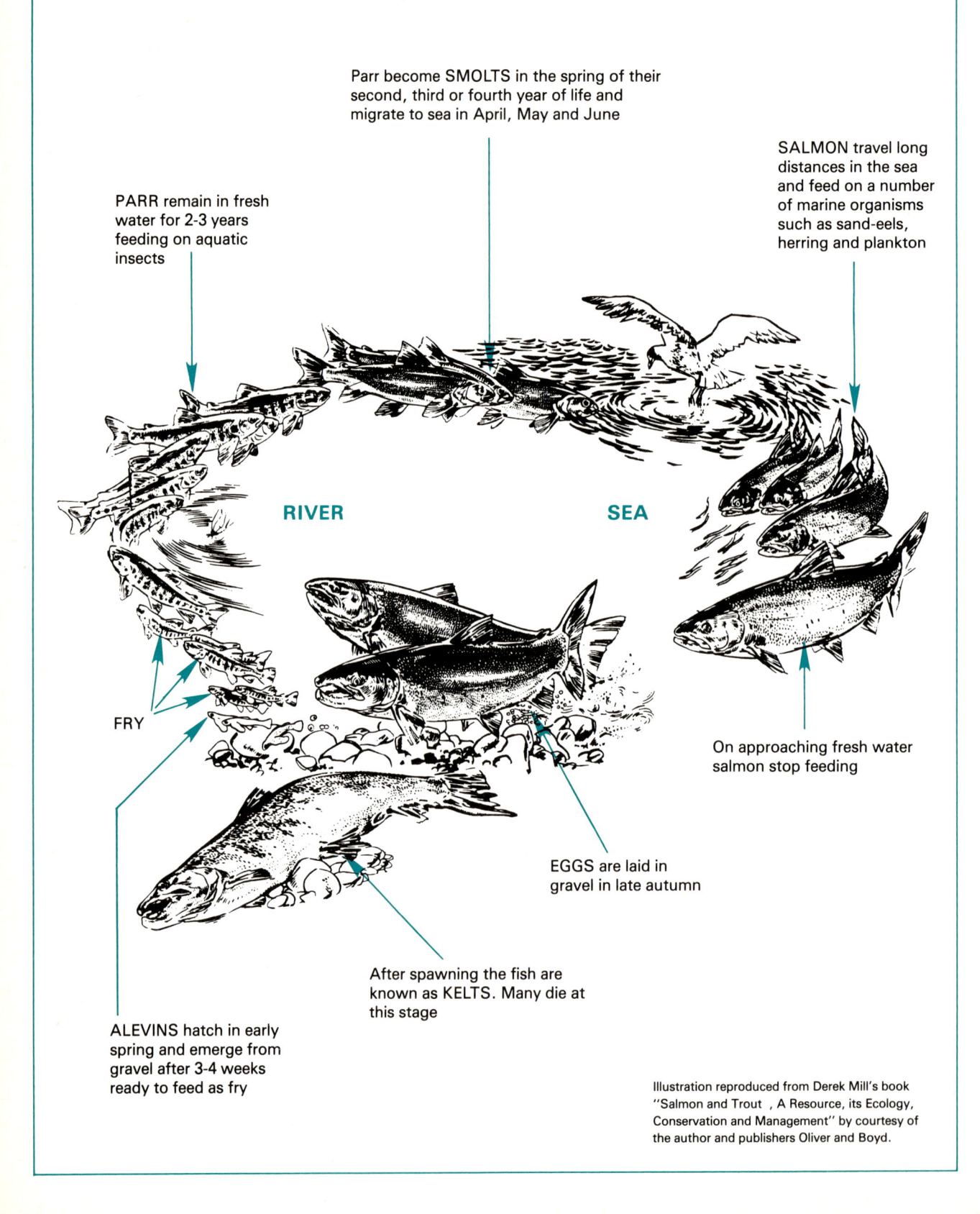

PARR remain in fresh water for 2-3 years feeding on aquatic insects

Parr become SMOLTS in the spring of their second, third or fourth year of life and migrate to sea in April, May and June

SALMON travel long distances in the sea and feed on a number of marine organisms such as sand-eels, herring and plankton

RIVER

SEA

FRY

On approaching fresh water salmon stop feeding

EGGS are laid in gravel in late autumn

After spawning the fish are known as KELTS. Many die at this stage

ALEVINS hatch in early spring and emerge from gravel after 3-4 weeks ready to feed as fry

Illustration reproduced from Derek Mill's book "Salmon and Trout, A Resource, its Ecology, Conservation and Management" by courtesy of the author and publishers Oliver and Boyd.

Impact on the Ecosystem and Nature Conservation (Continued)

- smolts normally stay near the surface and may resist the downward flow of the water and thus avoid the turbines. Without fish passes the only means of passing down through the barrage would then be via the ship locks and the sluices against the flood tide. Fish passes might deal with the problem. If available, these could also assist upstream migration of fish by being operated not only during the flood tide but also at the beginning of the ebb tide before the generating head has developed. If some of these fish passes were to be incorporated into the turbine caissons they would be well placed to assist upstream passage of those fish attracted by the turbulence of the turbine discharge during the previous generating cycle.
- if the migration of smolt shoals can be shown to be predictable and trackable it might be possible to open some of the sluices for short periods in the ebb tide to allow them to pass through. This would of course result in some loss of energy output.
- improved treatment of effluent into the Usk might be needed to maintain it as a salmon river and to allow the passage of other migratory fish. Alternatively, it may be preferable to divert effluent into the main Severn Estuary.

240. The Outer Barrage might adversely affect the movement of sea-trout to important rivers in South East Wales. It might, however, give some benefit to marine fish, though these are relatively unimportant in the Severn area.

Other Impacts on the Ecosystem

241. A development on this scale would have an extensive impact on the environment over much of the Severn Estuary area. Reductions in tidal amplitude would leave areas of saltmarsh permanently exposed which would become maritime grassland; there could be some extension of the lower saltmarsh. Where salinity is reduced upstream and in areas with a high water table, reed beds would develop. Careful management of such areas could result in the creation of interesting new habitats, but these would not directly compensate for saltmarsh lost.

242. Less information is available on intertidal hard substrata, subtidal habitats, marine fish and mammals, and seabirds. However, there would be changes in the habitats resulting in linked changes in the distribution of plants and animals. In general, the area upstream of a barrage would become more "estuarine" with a reduction in the marine component, while marine organisms presently below the proposed barrage would probably penetrate further up the estuary. The present pattern of gradation of species and habitats up the estuary would be altered, some new and alternative habitats being created as others disappear. An Outer Barrage would have a greater effect than an Inner Barrage, even with a second stage.

Impact on Sites of Geological Importance

243. Much of the geological interest in the coastal sites is located in wavecut platforms lying between high and low water marks. At present continual erosion prevents any undue accumulation of debris which would obscure the rock outcrops. Also, some of the sites are only accessible at low tide. Thus a decrease in the tidal amplitude would change the necessary erosion pattern and result in some sites being permanently underwater. The important Lilstock-Blue Anchor coastal site would be sensitive to any change of low water level. This implies that it would be adversely affected by the Outer Barrage or the second basin of the Staged Scheme but not by the Inner Barrage.

244. Some coastal sites could also suffer minor landslip, whilst some inland sites might be affected by quarrying.

Fig 45 Comparison of Leading Barrage Schemes

Item	Outer Barrage	Inner Barrage	Staged Scheme Stage I	Staged Scheme Stage II	Staged Scheme Overall†
SCHEME DESCRIPTION					
No. of 9 m Turbines	300	160	160	125	285
Generator Capacity MW	40	45	45	40	—
Total Installed Capacity MW	12,000	7,200	7,200	5,000	12,200
No. of 12 m Sluice equivalents	320	150	150	100	250
ENERGY AND ECONOMICS					
Energy Output, TWh/y, +14 -5%	19.7	12.9	10.4	7.7	18.1
Approx. Firm Capacity Contribution, MW	1,300	1,100			2,100
Acceptability of energy to system	+	+ +			+ + +
Raw Generation Cost, p/kWh, +5 -17%	3.6	3.1			3.8
Capital Cost, £M, +6 -10%	8,860	5,660	5,660	4,760	10,420
Benefit/Cost Ratio					
Scenario I	0.90	1.10	1.10	0.65	0.95
Scenario II	1.25	1.40	1.40	0.70	1.15
Scenario III	0.85	0.95	0.95	0.55	0.80
ENGINEERING					
Construction time, years					
— to first generation	13	9	9	8	9
— to full power generation	17	12	12	11	23
Opportunity for experience to be included	○	○			+ +
Difficulty/exposure	– – –	–			– –
IMPACTS					
Reduction in mean tidal range just outside the barrage	20%	11%	24%*	15%	
Port access	– – –	–			– –
Employment	+ +	+			+ + +
Recreation	+ + +	+ + +			+ + +
Water quality	– – –	–			– –
Power station cooling	–	○			– –
Transmission lines	– – –	–			– –
Sediments	?	?	?	?	?
Migratory fish	–	–			– –
Wading birds and shelduck	– – –	–			– –
Remainder of the ecosystem	– – –	–			– –
Amenity:					
— Landfalls (Welsh/English)	– / – –	– / – –			– / – – –
— Earth Science Sites	– –	–			– –

Notes:
1.   + + + most benefit   + + medium benefit   + least benefit   ○ very little impact
       – – – most disbenefit   – – medium disbenefit   – least disbenefit   ? impact uncertain
2. The + and – impacts are consistent across a row but are not intended to relate to the relative magnitude and importance of different impacts.
3. All costs are shown in December 1980 £.
4. † Assumes that construction of Stage II starts on completion of Stage I.
5. * This is the tidal range reduction outside the Stage I Barrage when Stage II is complete.

Comparison of Leading Schemes 23

245. So far we have discussed the many separate issues which could affect a decision on the barrage. It is now appropriate to compare the information assembled on each of the three leading barrage schemes to see whether there is sufficient evidence to make a definitive choice between them. The schemes to be compared are:

(a) **An Outer Barrage** running from east of Minehead to Aberthaw. This large ebb generation scheme would effectively develop the full energy potential of the estuary and would require only one political decision.

(b) **An Inner Barrage** running from Brean Down to the vicinity of Lavernock Point. This ebb generation scheme would give nearly two-thirds of the energy output of the Outer Scheme. It would be the most economic in giving the greatest return for each pound invested.

(c) **A Staged Scheme,** the first stage being as (b) above and the second stage being an enclosure running from just off Brean Down to east of Minehead, encircling Bridgwater Bay. This scheme also effectively develops the full energy potential of the estuary and, provided the second stage generates on the flood tide, gives energy in a form more valuable to the CEGB system. However, its construction would require two decisions the second of which would require more difficult economic and environmental problems to be faced.

246. These schemes can be compared on technical and economic grounds, and by considering their various impacts on man and the environment, as shown in Fig 45. However, it is not possible to quantify all the issues involved and a grading system showing the relative impact has been used. It does not quantify the relative importance of each type of impact as many of these judgements are subjective in character.

Economics

247. Preliminary studies suggest that the Inner Barrage could meet the Treasury's minimum requirement of a 5% return on investment if the proportion of nuclear plant in the generating system rises only to a limited extent. The Outer Barrage and Staged Scheme show performances which are both about 15% worse, being fully viable only if the rate of growth of nuclear plant is constrained below about 1 GW/year. Although there are still uncertainties in both barrage costs and the future value of energy, further studies are considered unlikely to change the view that the Inner Barrage is the most economic of these three options.

248. The main economic advantage of the Staged Scheme compared with the Outer Barrage is that it enables a phased approach to exploitation of the estuary, reducing the financial commitment and risk at any one time. However, when considered as a separate investment the second stage would not be economically attractive on present costings.

Engineering

249. The Staged Scheme has a clear advantage over the Outer Barrage in that experience gained in the construction of the first stage can be applied to the design and construction of the second stage.

250. A staged approach would also reduce the pressure on resources of materials and labour for construction, spreading employment over a greater period, and on manufacturing industry for turbines, switchgear, etc.

251. The Inner Barrage is seen as the most prudent undertaking as regards the length and degree of exposure of the structure and the difficulty of achieving "closure". The Staged Scheme has the appearance of being more complicated than the Outer Barrage, but should nevertheless result in fewer risks and greater security of energy output.

Impacts

252. In most cases where adverse impacts are likely to occur, present evidence indicates that these would be least severe with the Inner Barrage and most severe with the Outer Barrage, with the Staged Scheme having an intermediate impact, e.g.:

Port Access The Inner Barrage would have a smaller effect on maximum water levels at the ports. The Outer Barrage and Staged Scheme would both result in a greater reduction in maximum water levels. The difference in water levels between the Inner and Outer Barrage is likely to be modest in absolute terms (about ½m), but navigation studies have shown that at neap tides this difference would be important.

Land Drainage Above the Holm Islands, all schemes would have similar effects, which are regarded as a modest disbenefit caused by extra pumping and a modest benefit caused by a reduction in extreme sea levels. In Bridgwater Bay the Outer Barrage would produce the same effects as above the Holm Islands. The second stage of the Staged Scheme would produce clear benefits in terms of land drainage and sea defence levels, although this could be to the detriment of nature conservation interests in wetland areas.

Water Quality in the Estuary Any increase in conservative pollutants, including potentially harmful ones like cadmium, would be more marked for the Outer than for the Inner Barrage. With the Outer Barrage the change in salinity would also be greater and, although this is not significant in the context of water quality, it would have implications for the ecosystem and nature conservation.

Sediments All schemes are likely to reduce the average rate of sediment transport both behind and just in front of a barrage, as a result of generally slower water currents. However, there is insufficient evidence at present to make any relative judgements between the schemes on this aspect.

Power Station Cooling The Outer Barrage could affect Aberthaw power station. The second stage of the Staged Scheme could affect Hinkley Point. In both cases, remedial works might be needed.

Wading Birds and Shelduck The largest area of intertidal flats would be lost with the Outer Barrage. The Inner Barrage would have much less impact on the internationally important Bridgwater Bay than either of the other schemes.

Migratory Fish The Inner and Outer Barrages would obstruct to a similar extent the passage of migratory fish heading towards the sea. The second stage could cause fish migrating upstream to be diverted from their true direction by being drawn through the working turbines. These factors are still being studied.

Conclusion

253. The Inner Barrage is the most attractive scheme because it would minimise engineering risks, have least impact on man and the environment, and be the most cost-effective. Although it would not fully exploit the energy potential of the estuary, this could be achieved by building a second stage, if at a later date this should be considered desirable.

Fig 46 15 Year Programme for the Inner Barrage

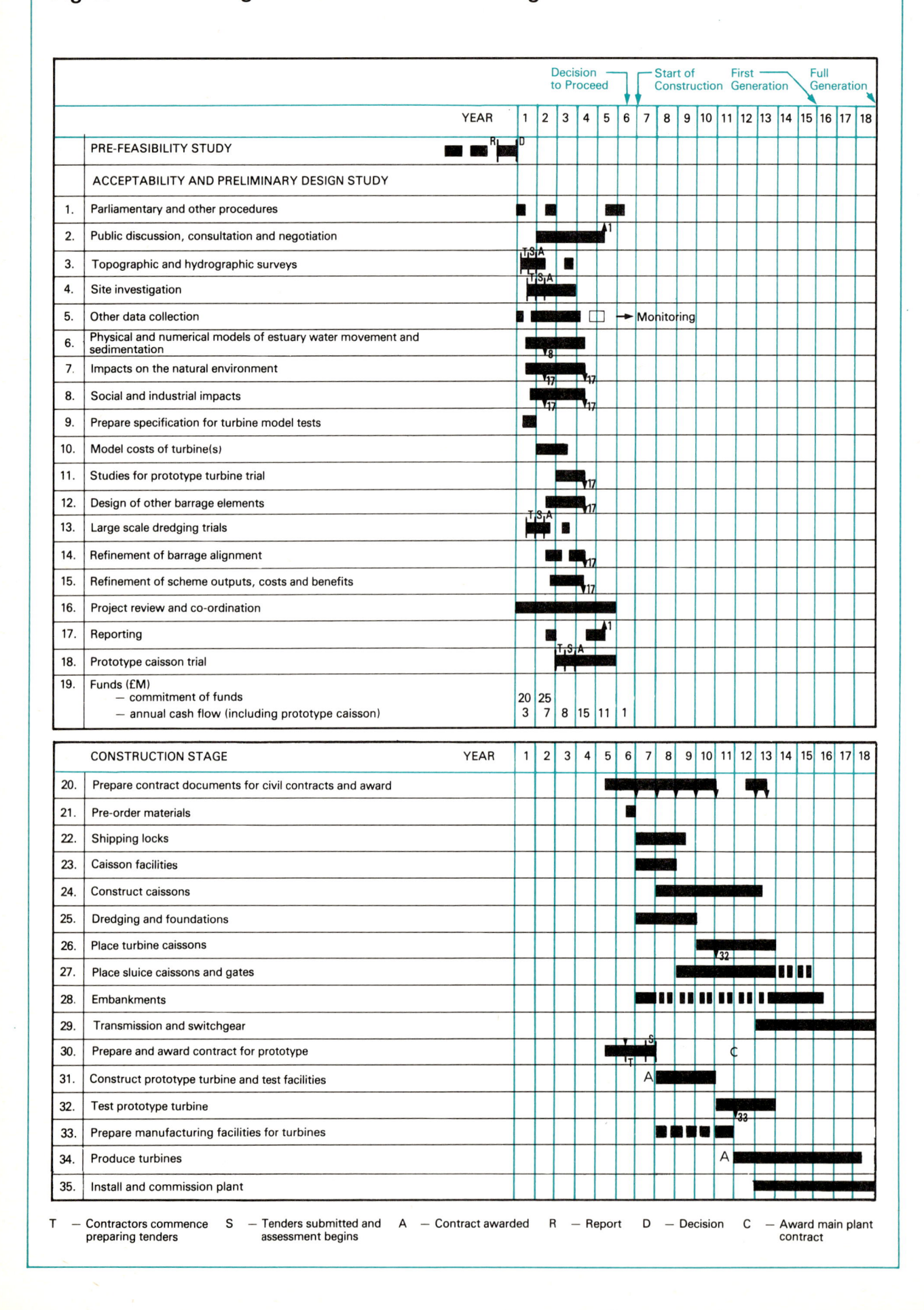

	YEAR	1	2	3	4	5	6	7	8	9	10	11	12	13	14	15	16	17	18
	PRE-FEASIBILITY STUDY																		
	ACCEPTABILITY AND PRELIMINARY DESIGN STUDY																		
1.	Parliamentary and other procedures																		
2.	Public discussion, consultation and negotiation																		
3.	Topographic and hydrographic surveys																		
4.	Site investigation																		
5.	Other data collection							Monitoring											
6.	Physical and numerical models of estuary water movement and sedimentation																		
7.	Impacts on the natural environment																		
8.	Social and industrial impacts																		
9.	Prepare specification for turbine model tests																		
10.	Model costs of turbine(s)																		
11.	Studies for prototype turbine trial																		
12.	Design of other barrage elements																		
13.	Large scale dredging trials																		
14.	Refinement of barrage alignment																		
15.	Refinement of scheme outputs, costs and benefits																		
16.	Project review and co-ordination																		
17.	Reporting																		
18.	Prototype caisson trial																		
19.	Funds (£M) — commitment of funds — annual cash flow (including prototype caisson)	20 / 3	25 / 7	/ 8	/ 15	/ 11	/ 1												

Decision to Proceed — year 5/6
Start of Construction — year 6/7
First Generation — year 12
Full Generation — year 15

	CONSTRUCTION STAGE	YEAR	1	2	3	4	5	6	7	8	9	10	11	12	13	14	15	16	17	18
20.	Prepare contract documents for civil contracts and award																			
21.	Pre-order materials																			
22.	Shipping locks																			
23.	Caisson facilities																			
24.	Construct caissons																			
25.	Dredging and foundations																			
26.	Place turbine caissons																			
27.	Place sluice caissons and gates																			
28.	Embankments																			
29.	Transmission and switchgear																			
30.	Prepare and award contract for prototype																			
31.	Construct prototype turbine and test facilities																			
32.	Test prototype turbine																			
33.	Prepare manufacturing facilities for turbines																			
34.	Produce turbines																			
35.	Install and commission plant																			

T — Contractors commence preparing tenders   S — Tenders submitted and assessment begins   A — Contract awarded   R — Report   D — Decision   C — Award main plant contract

The Way Ahead 24

The Case for Further Study

254. It is clear from the work which has been done as part of this study that a tidal power scheme could be constructed which would be economic in the sense that it would show a rate of return greater than the 5% minimum currently required by Treasury for investment in the public sector. The Inner Barrage is likely to show a benefit to cost ratio close to or greater than unity over a number of possible views of the future. However, a key question is whether tidal power is sufficiently economic to be chosen against nuclear power, which can also save fossil fuel.

255. Fig 22 gives the comparative figures for a possible investment decision which might enable a tidal power station or a nuclear power station to come on stream around the turn of the century. If the assumptions used in the economic model are correct, then it is clear that on the basis of economic analysis alone, one would not wish to invest in tidal power as a first choice.

256. However, there are doubts whether the nuclear programme now projected will be achieved, and also current cost estimates must involve uncertainties. As for the first, public acceptability is an acknowledged matter of concern, both in general and in relation to the necessary power station sites. This concern could also affect cost estimates for nuclear power, if this should lead to a proliferation of safety measures. These estimates are also dependent on the eventual flexibility and availability of nuclear plant and on the ability of industry to build, deliver and commission complex machinery within cost and time schedules. Moreover, neither the future availability of uranium, nor its future price, nor the eventual cost and acceptability of fast reactors can now be forecast with assurance.

257. Further investment in nuclear power could therefore be constrained or be markedly less attractive than now envisaged. In such circumstances investment in tidal power would be economically attractive.

258. In conclusion, there are a number of possible future developments which, although not coinciding with the Committee's central view, are utterly conceivable and would result in nuclear power either becoming restricted or unexpectedly expensive. Indeed, in any conceivable future in which electricity might be expensive, a barrage could form an important component of the country's generating system, since its operating costs would continue to be very low indeed once the capital outlay has been made. A barrage could thus provide valuable *insurance* against futures in which energy is unexpectedly expensive.

259. In addition, there could be some merit in increasing the *diversity* of generating plant within the electricity supply system to improve security of supply. However, the value of this is difficult to quantify.

260. The Committee believes that in these circumstances an Acceptability and Preliminary Design Study should be undertaken forthwith. The main aims of this study would be the establishment of the economic and environmental acceptability of the Inner Barrage. It would also include further data collection and studies aimed at optimising the various elements of barrage design and estuary closure.

261. This study would increase confidence in the benefits, direct and indirect costs and acceptability of a barrage to the point where an early decision to go ahead could be made. Proceeding with such a study now would have the advantage of reducing by four years the lead time for realisation of a barrage, thus raising tidal power closer to the status of an "off-the-shelf" technology. This could be achieved for the comparatively modest sum of about £20M.

Fig 47 Acceptability and Preliminary Design Study — Summary of Costs

Item	Subject	Cost (£k) Engineering Studies	Environmental Studies
1	Discussion, consultation and publicity		300
2	Topographic and hydrographic surveys	50	350
3	Site investigation	750	
4	Other data collection	370	2,830
5	Physical and numerical models	400	1,500
6	Impacts on the natural environment		2,000
7	Social and industrial impacts		700
8	Specification of turbine model tests	100	
9	Model tests of turbines	750	
10	Studies for prototype turbine trial	375	25
11	Design of other barrage elements	1,300	50
12	Large scale dredging trials	1,000	
13	Refinement of barrage alignment	150	50
14	Refinement of scheme outputs, costs and benefits	400	50
15	Project review	450	250
16	Reporting	80	120
17	Design work for caisson prototype trial	995	55
		7,170	8,280

Sub total 15,450
Allowance for other work not yet specified 4,550
£20,000,000

In addition, for the 15 year programme there is an option after two years for:

Prototype trials of turbine caissons £25,000,000

TOTAL £45,000,000

The Way Ahead (Continued)

Future Programmes

262. A range of different programmes and decision sequences can be postulated for a Severn Barrage. At one extreme, a decision to build an Inner Barrage as soon as possible with an overlapping programme of studies, design and building could result in first electricity generation within 10 years.

263. A second option is a fully sequential staged programme. This would consist of an Acceptability and Preliminary Design Study followed by public discussion, a decision to build, caisson and turbine trials and finally barrage construction, all taken step by step. This would take about 20 years to first electricity generation.

264. A third option is a middle course (Fig 46), which would require a period of 15 years from the start of a four year acceptability study to electricity being produced. Crucial to this programme is the taking of a decision to proceed with prototype caisson trials half way through the next phase of study. Information would then be available from a physical model of the estuary and a numerical water movement model, as well as from various environmental studies, which would all be relevant to any decision to proceed with caisson trials prior to a commitment to construct the barrage.

265. A first estimate of the content and cost of an acceptability and preliminary Design Study is summarised in Fig 47.

266. The Committee's view is that the first option of a 10 year "crash" programme for construction is not appropriate, since this would require an immediate decision to build a barrage before its acceptability is established. The second option of a 20 year programme appears unnecessarily long and could reduce the credibility of tidal power as an energy resource. The Committee therefore recommend that a start be made on the 15 year programme. This would involve an initial commitment of £20M for a four year acceptability and preliminary Design Study. After two years of this study a decision would be required on whether to proceed with prototype caisson trials at an additional cost of around £25M. There would be some financial risk in making a commitment to caisson trials before the acceptability study is fully complete, but taking this risk would enable power to be obtained substantially earlier. The decision to bring forward caisson trials would require a policy decision by Government as to whether this risk could be accepted.

Fig 48 Proposed Acceptability Programme. Breakdown of Environmental, Social & Industrial studies

Data Collection
- Tide data (part allocation)
- Current data
- Suspended sediments
- Bottom sediments
- Water quality sampling
- Invertebrate densities and distributions
- Plant survey (foreshore and sub-tidal)
- Inland surveys (wetlands etc that may be affected)
- Fish populations, spawning grounds etc (non-migratory)
- Migratory fish, including tracking
- Wading birds, seasonal counts etc
- Recreation, existing patterns etc
- Employment (survey skills and availability)
- Materials (availability, transport and costs)

Physical and Numerical Models of Estuary Water Movement and Sedimentation
- 2-D model of Western Approaches
- 2-D model of Severn Estuary Water Movements
- 2-D layered model of Severn Estuary (water movement, sediment transport, salinity and pollution)
- Physical model of Severn Estuary

Impacts on the Natural Environment
- Numerical models of water quality and ecosystem
- Numerical models of dispersion at sewage and cooling water outfals including design of remedial measures
- Assess impact of barrage on water quality
- Study behaviour of wading birds and shelduck
- Migratory fish studies
- Ecology of saltmarshes
- Studies of fundamental processes as input to studies of specific species and habitats
- Outline costing of land drainage and sea defence
- Environmental management options including study of new or alternative habitats
- Nature conservation assessment
- Management and coordination of environmental studies

Social and Industrial Impacts
- Refine recreation benefits and costs
- Assess effects of barrage construction and operation on each port
- Road link over barrage
- Assess value of employment, redeployment of labour etc
- Assess planning implications, land use, effects of construction traffic, work camps etc
- Overall study of regional implications of a barrage

Conclusions and Recommendations 25

267. A Severn Barrage would by any standards of comparison be a very large scheme. Not only is one talking about costs of several billions of pounds, but the size of the area affected, the amount of material and scale of engineering required, and the potential environmental impact would be uniquely large. It is clear that decision taking on undertakings of this kind must be done in stages. This is especially true of the Severn Barrage because of the range and extent of its potential effects.

Summary of Progress

268. The Severn Barrage Committee has met eleven times over the last two and a half years. During this time the Committee's Technical Secretariat has commissioned some £2.3M of studies enabling much progress to be made in:

- understanding the practicalities and problems of all types of tidal power schemes
- collecting appropriate environmental and engineering data
- developing, proving and using models of tidal movements and energy outputs
- assessing the economic value of the electrical output of a barrage to the generating system
- identifying the environmental effects of a barrage
- narrowing down the choice of schemes and elements within them
- identifying the remaining problems to be studied.

269. Following these studies the Committee's view is that the economic prospect for tidal power in the Severn Estuary has improved, since about 40% more energy than was reported four years ago in Energy Papers 23 and 27 is now forseen for the same capital outlay. It is now thought likely that the building of a tidal barrage could reduce the overall cost of electricity generation, if the proportion of nuclear plant in the generating system does not rise rapidly. However, if the option is available, building additional nuclear plant would, on present estimates, be an economically better investment. Nevertheless, tidal power should be viewed as a valuable supplementary source of electricity supply, and is indeed leading among the renewable sources of energy.

270. The Committee has found that:—

(i) the technical feasibility of a barrage is not in doubt.

(ii) the economic justification for a barrage is dependent on a number of factors (such as the extent of nuclear generation of electricity and the price of coal during the first third of the next century) which cannot be known when a decision on whether to go forward is taken. However, the barrage would be so valuable in any future in which this country faced serious energy problems *that the Committee unanimously recommends that a further phase of work should be undertaken forthwith.*

(iii) the environmental consequences of a barrage would be so wide ranging that they need to be studied in much greater depth than the time and money available to us allowed. Thus, in this next phase these matters must be investigated very fully, especially the consequences of barrage design on port access, sewage disposal, recreation, bird life, salmon fisheries, land drainage and so on. Environmental considerations are an essential part of the barrage decision.

Conclusions and Recommendations (Continued)

The Value of Tidal Power and Economic Viability of a Barrage

271. The chief argument for a barrage is the economic value of the electricity generated by it. All other economic considerations, such as road crossing and potential recreational benefits, are either relatively unimportant or too speculative to be likely to affect any decision whether or not to proceed.

272. Estimating the value of the electricity generated is complex. We have done this by looking at the electricity supply system optimised with or without a barrage over the relevant period (say 2000-2030, as later benefits would be heavily discounted and thus have low net present value) and trying to estimate which of these is the more advantageous.

273. Tidal power is like nuclear power in that the capital costs dominate, with the operating costs being small by comparison. However, although tidal power is predictable, a barrage is unlike any form of thermal power station in that the timing and size of its input to the grid are controlled not by the need for power but by the daily and monthly rhythms of the tides. Thus the contribution of tidal power to saving capital investment in power stations would be relatively modest, its value being primarily the value of other fuel (coal, oil, uranium) that it would displace. Since uranium fuel is likely to remain the cheapest of these, and oil is unlikely to be important in the period in question, the justification of the capital cost of a barrage must be based largely on the value of the coal it would displace. Nuclear stations, with their low running costs would, of course, be used as much as possible.

274. One can then divide the possible future into three conceivable cases:*

Case 1 is defined as a future in which there is a very substantial amount of nuclear electricity generation. So large a part of the generating capacity is nuclear that, for more than 25% of the time, no significant amount of generation by fossil fuelled plant takes place. In such a case, the Barrage would displace coal for less than 75% of the time only, and otherwise displace nuclear electricity with its low operating costs. Therefore, in such conditions, the Barrage would be uneconomic by any criterion.

Case 2. In this future, the nuclear component of the generating system is not so high and, for more than 75% of the time, substantial coal burning takes place. Thus for most of the time operation of the Barrage would displace coal. While there are great uncertainties about the price of coal in the next century, our expectation is that, in such circumstances, an optimised Barrage would show the required 5% rate of return on investment and would therefore be economic in this sense. This does not imply a judgement that there are not more economic ways of generating electricity. Indeed, the most economic use of capital to lower the cost of electricity might then not be to build a Barrage but to build more nuclear power stations.

Case 3. This is a future, not our central view but utterly conceivable, in which energy is unexpectedly expensive. This could occur in a number of ways. For example, if the growth of the nuclear component is restricted by a lack of acceptability of nuclear power or a shortage of uranium coupled with failure of the fast breeder reactor to succeed in its economy or its acceptability, then this is likely to be a worldwide phenomenon with a marked effect on the price of coal. This would effectively exclude the most economic option of building further nuclear power stations and thus make the barrage an economically attractive investment. In this case the barrage would be a most important component of the country's generating capacity, since its operating costs would continue to be very low once the capital outlay has been made.

---

*Note: These cases are not the same as Scenarios I, II and III described in paragraph 113.

Conclusions and Recommendations (Continued)

275. Thus, our overall conclusion is that a barrage would be a valuable insurance against the blackest kind of energy future. This insurance would involve substantial investment but would give a real return of better than 5% if nuclear electricity generation does not become a very high proportion of the total. Provided that for over, say, 75% of the time nuclear generation would need to be supplemented by significant fossil fuel burn, then during these periods tidal power with its low operating cost would displace expensive coal or oil rather than cheap uranium fuel.

276. Moreover, a barrage would add to the diversity of sources of electric power. This would reduce the risk of system failure if, through discovery of a type fault in conventional generating plant or for other reasons, there should be a temporary scarcity of electricity generating capacity. It would also reduce the risks due to temporary shortages of power station fuels. However, this benefit of tidal power is difficult to quantify.

277. All in all, these arguments convinced the Committee that it would be most unwise not to proceed immediately to the investigations that are required to reach a position where Government can responsibly decide whether to build a barrage.

Preferred Schemes

278. There are a number of options available for the siting of the barrage. Within limits, the further west the barrage is built the larger is the volume of enclosed water and the greater the energy available. On the other hand the tidal range reduces so that the power output does not rise in proportion. Also the engineering costs rise. There are, however, distinct optima in the geography which are discussed below.

279. Furthermore the nature and mode of operation of a barrage have to be chosen. Single basin schemes do not permit significant freedom from the timetable set by tidal movements although, depending on the chosen mode of operation and design of the turbines, they can generate electricity either during the ebb or the flood flow, or both. For a barrage across the estuary an ebb generation scheme is preferred, because it would minimise the unit cost of electricity generation and have less effect on the ports than flood or two-way generation.

280. Certain types of double-basin scheme could also be used to store energy. However, energy storage in the Severn Estuary would be considerably more expensive than other alternative options and the Committee have firmly concluded that utilisation of the estuary for energy storage would be economically unattractive.

281. Concentrating then on ebb generation schemes, there is an optimal siting of the barrage between Brean Down (just south of Weston-super-Mare) and the Welsh Coast in the vicinity of Lavernock Point, enclosing both Flat Holm and Steep Holm. This Inner Barrage would give the highest energy output per unit of capital invested. Indeed, with reasonable assumptions about the cost of the barrage and about the (much more uncertain) price of coal next century, with nuclear power restricted so that some coal fired plant is working at almost all times, there would be a real rate of return exceeding 5%. The economic optimum design for such a barrage would have an installed capacity of 7,200 GW, with an annual output of nearly 13 TWh.

Conclusions and Recommendations (Continued)

282. An alternative would be an Outer Barrage, maximising energy output from the estuary. The optimal line for such a scheme would run due north from a point just east of Minehead. Although this scheme would have nearly twice as many turbines as the Inner Barrage, its energy output would only be about 50% greater and hence its economic performance would be lower. The Committee was daunted by the scale of this scheme. It was also concerned about both the greater engineering risks and the much larger area affected and therefore the scale of environmental impact. For these reasons the Committee firmly recommends that attention should be concentrated on the Inner Barrage.

283. Another way of obtaining this larger amount of energy would be to develop the estuary in stages. Construction of the Inner Barrage could be followed by a second barrage running from a point on the Inner Barrage just west of Brean Down to just east of Minehead, enclosing Bridgwater Bay. The second basin of this Staged Scheme might be again of the ebb generation type, maximising its power output. However, it would probably be more attractive to run it in flood generation mode so that this second barrage would deliver power to the grid at times other than when the first barrage was generating. Flood generation there might also mitigate the potentially disturbing environmental impact on Bridgwater Bay. However, on present costings the addition of a second basin to the Inner Barrage would not be attractive economically.

Environmental, Social and Industrial Impacts

284. The Committee was most concerned about the potential environmental, social and industrial impacts of a barrage. In the time and with the money available we could not do much more than identify possible impacts, make some preliminary judgements and suggest further work which would be required to clarify difficult areas. However, it was our firm intent that our list of potential impacts should be as complete as possible. Above all, we decided that a further stage of Severn Barrage endeavours would need to concentrate more resources than we had available to us on resolving the numerous environmental, social and industrial questions involved, both positive and negative.

285. To begin with those effects most directly linked to current economic activities, there is the question of port access. The ability of the ports in the Severn Estuary to accept sizeable ships is itself only due to the exceptionally high tides of the Bristol Channel. The heights of the tides at the port entrances following the construction of a barrage would be critical for the continued accessibility of the ports.

286. Although with such a major change in the estuary some uncertainty must remain, hydraulic modelling experts believe that the tidal regime following construction of a barrage can now be predicted to about one foot. This level of uncertainty is just about tolerable to the port authorities, provided the central predicted level is not too near the critical level. Equally the future navigability of the estuary will depend on changes in siltation regime and the position of the sand banks, which of course have never been entirely stable. Further and deeper studies would throw much light on these without necessarily being able to attain absolute certainty. Compared with these issues the definition of the size, positioning and number of ship locks is a relatively minor and easily estimated part of the overall barrage costs.

Conclusions and Recommendations (Continued)

287. Next one comes to the questions of effluent disposal, quality of tidal waters, land drainage and sea defence. There is no doubt that, at a price which we estimate to be equivalent to 5-10% of the construction cost of the barrage, conditions could generally be restored to those existing, but the timing and scale of the necessary engineering works would require significant further study. We are confident that, following such deeper study, no major technical uncertainties would remain. On the question of estuarine water quality, construction of a barrage would lead to generally gentler currents and therefore reduce dispersion of effluents. Greater care would therefore be needed in treating effluents discharged into the estuary. However, the need for and extent of any additional treatment would depend on policies being adopted at the time for quality of tidal waters.

288. Modifying the barrage to carry a public road across the estuary would cost about the same as duplicating the present Severn Bridge. However, there would be substantial additional costs, both financial and environmental, in providing the necessary access roads. Such a crossing might be of less use to traffic than a second bridge, but could have socio-economic advantages in linking areas which at present have poor road communication.

289. In addition the construction of a barrage could have a significant impact on the tourist attractions of the estuary, particularly since the much reduced tidal range within the barrage would affect the coastal resorts upstream of it. Which of the effects would be positive and which negative is difficult to decide at this stage. The opportunities in the area for recreation and boating, now small because of the large tidal currents and the lack of marinas, could be markedly enhanced within the basin, perhaps utilising some of the facilities provided for barrage construction.

290. There are also a number of other social and industrial considerations. The importance of a barrage for employment and the future development of industry around the estuary, will need further investigation. A barrage would have impacts on land resources and local communities, especially during the construction stage. The effect of a barrage on existing amenities will also need careful consideration.

291. Clearly the fisheries of the area would be affected. The value particularly of the salmon fisheries is substantial and present knowledge of how to ensure that these are not adversely affected is limited. There is, however, reasonable optimism that for modest expense it would be possible to enable fish migration to continue through the barrage. The damage to these fisheries could therefore be made slight, but this would need to be established more firmly during the next study phase.

292. Finally the inter-tidal banks of the estuary have considerable importance for wildlife in general, particularly the mud flats of Bridgwater Bay (which may or may not be affected according to the siting of the barrage). These are the subject of international obligations and are of major interest in ecological respects. We would not expect a barrage to have a significant effect on wild life near the head of the estuary.

Conclusions and Recommendations (Continued)

Recommendations

293. The Committee recommends that attention should be concentrated on the Inner Barrage. This is the most attractive scheme because it would have the least engineering risk and the least adverse impact on man and the environment and would be the most cost-effective. The Committee does not believe that the sole attraction of the Outer Barrage, its larger energy output, would outweigh the greater engineering risks, more adverse environmental impacts and marginally worse economics.

294. Building the Inner Barrage would leave open the option of fully utilising the energy potential of the estuary by constructing a second stage basin to its South-West. However, on present costings this option would not be economically attractive and would have its own environmental problems. A decision on this option could be made independently at any time.

295. The Committee finds that the Inner Barrage is likely to be economically attractive if nuclear electricity generation capacity remains limited and also has real insurance value against a future in which energy costs are unexpectedly high. Since the Committee is greatly concerned by the as yet imperfectly understood impacts of a barrage, it feels strongly that it must recommend early setting in train of deeper studies to establish the acceptability of the Inner Barrage. These would include investigation of environmental, social and industrial factors coupled with preliminary design and further economic evaluation. The aim would be to put Government as soon as possible in a position where it could responsibly decide, in the light of all relevant factors, whether to authorise the building of a barrage.

296. The Committee believes that such a combined *Acceptability and Preliminary Design Study* for the Inner Barrage, building on present efforts, should not take more than four years or cost more than £20M. Halfway through this study a decision would be needed on whether to proceed with handling and foundation trials of a prototype caisson in the estuary at a further cost of about £25M. Although these trials are not required to establish the acceptability of a barrage, bringing them forward in this way would substantially shorten the overall time to first electricity generation.

ANNEX ONE: TERMS OF REFERENCE FOR THE SEVERN BARRAGE COMMITTEE

1. The Fourth Report from the Select Committee on Science and Technology[1] recommended that an independent Committee, similar to the Severn Barrage Committee of 1925-33, be established with responsibility for further work on assessing Severn Barrage schemes and their feasibility. The Government accepted this recommendation and set up a Committee under the Chairmanship of the Chief Scientist of the Department of Energy, Sir Hermann Bondi, KCB, FRS, with the following terms of reference:[2]

> To advise and assist the Secretary of State for Energy in reaching a decision on whether to proceed with a scheme for harnessing the tidal energy of the Severn Estuary, in particular:—
>
> (a) to recommend what further work should be carried out to establish the advantages and disadvantages of possible schemes; and
> (b) to recommend, in the light of such work, whether or not to proceed with the construction of a scheme having regard to all relevant considerations including:
> (i) the energy that might be obtained
> (ii) its cost by comparison with other means of power generation and steps to conserve energy
> (iii) the impact on the coastal regime and the implications for the environment, transport systems and economy of the regions concerned.

2. The Committee held their first meeting in October 1978. Membership of the Committee is as follows:

Mr. B. H. Bailey, OBE, JP	Regional Secretary, South West TUC
Mr. G. M. Binnie, FRS	Consultant, Binnie and Partners
Mr. W. Bor, CBE	Architect; Consultant, Llewelyn-Davies Weeks
Mr. W. P. Davey	Chief Executive, South Glamorgan County Council
Councillor C. Draper	Member, Bristol City Council
Professor R. W. Edwards	Head of Department of Applied Biology at the University of Wales Institute of Science and Technology
Professor Sir Hugh Ford, FRS	Professor of Mechanical Engineering, University of London (Imperial College)
Captain R. A. Gibbons	Haven Master and Conservancy Officer, Port of Bristol Authority
Mr. J. C. Heywood	Chief Executive, Horstmann Gear Co. Ltd., Bath
Mr. D. Jones	Chief Engineer, British Transport Docks Board
Mr. J. A. Jukes, CB	Member, Central Electricity Generating Board (now retired)
Professor G. V. T. Matthews	Director of Research and Deputy Director of the Wildfowl Trust
Sir Alec Merrison, DL, FRS	Vice Chancellor, University of Bristol
Professor R. Millward	Professor and Chairman of the Department of Economics, University of Salford
Mr. R. Morgan	Industrial Development Officer, South Glamorgan County Council
Mr. A. Palmer, MP	Member of Parliament for Bristol North East, Chairman, Select Committee on Science and Technology
Councillor G. Powell	Member, Gwent County Council
Mr. J. G. Quicke, CBE	Farmer; former member of Economic Development Council on Agriculture
Mr. T. M. Haydn Rees, CBE, DL, JP	Chairman, Welsh Water Authority
Mr. O. G. Saunders, MBE	Member, General Council, Wales TUC
Sir Gervais Walker, JP	Chairman, Avon County Council
Sir John Wills, Bt, TD, JP	Chairman, Wessex Water Authority and Lord Lieutenant of Avon

---

1. Select Committee on Science and Technology. Fourth report, Session 1976-77. "The exploitation of tidal power in the Severn Estuary". HC. 564 HMSO. 1977.
2. Cmnd 7236, HMSO 1978, The Development of Alternative Sources of Energy.

ANNEX TWO: TERMS OF REFERENCE OF THE PRE-FEASIBILITY STUDY ON TIDAL POWER IN THE SEVERN ESTUARY

1. At their first meeting the Severn Barrage Committee recognised that further research and development on tidal power was necessary if it was to become a credible option which could be compared with other methods of electricity generation. A full scale feasibility study costing some tens of millions of pounds was not at that time considered justified because of the many uncertainties about the various schemes proposed. There were then major uncertainties about the technical feasibility of constructing a large barrage system, the likely cost, the likely benefits of incorporating a varying energy source into the supply system, and the possible impacts on man and the environment.

2. It was therefore considered prudent that a limited but well coordinated programme of studies, including cost sensitivity analyses of crucial factors, should be carried out prior to any commitment to a full scale research and development study. The aims of this initial pre-feasibility study were:—

    - to narrow the options to one or two schemes and sites
    - to select the best constructional approach for each option
    - generally to clarify the status of a tidal barrage among the renewable sources of energy.

3. During the course of the study it became clear that two further aims should be added:—

    - to clarify the status of tidal power against conventional sources such as coal and nuclear power, and to consider how it would fit into the electricity supply system.
    - to determine whether there are any insurmountable environmental objections.

4. In carrying out this pre-feasibility study it was considered necessary to restrict the scope and depth of work to that which would enable a report to be made within a timescale of two years and a budget of £1.5 millions. The budget was later increased to a total of £2.405 millions enabling a start to be made on some longer term studies.

ANNEX THREE: ROLE OF THE WORKING PARTY ON TIDAL POWER

1. The pre-feasibility study was carried out under the overall guidance of the Severn Barrage Committee with the Working Party on Tidal Power acting as its technical secretariat. Day to day management of the programme was carried out by the Energy Technology Support Unit at Harwell, assisted by independent professional advice from Binnie and Partners, a firm of consulting engineers experienced in coastal and estuarial projects. The main functions of the Working Party were to:

- advise SBC on the work which should be carried out to meet the terms of reference of the pre-feasibility study,
- advise the Department of Energy on the funding of individual projects within the study programme,
- assess the results of all studies as they became available,
- coordinate the results of individual projects in the overall pre-feasibility study programme,
- give technical advice to SBC as required,
- draft reports on behalf of the SBC,
- act as a forum for information and to enable the views of various Government departments to be discussed.

2. The Working Party met at approximately monthly intervals throughout the study period under the chairmanship of Dr. F. J. P. Clarke, Research Director for Energy, UKAEA Harwell.

3. Membership of the Working Party was made up of representatives from the following organisations:—

Department of Energy
Department of the Environment
Department of Industry
Ministry of Agriculture, Fisheries and Food
Welsh Office
Binnie and Partners
Central Electricity Generating Board
Energy Technology Support Unit, Harwell
University College, Cardiff (Dr. J.M. Edington)

Fig 49 Organisation of Pre-Feasibility Study Showing Participants

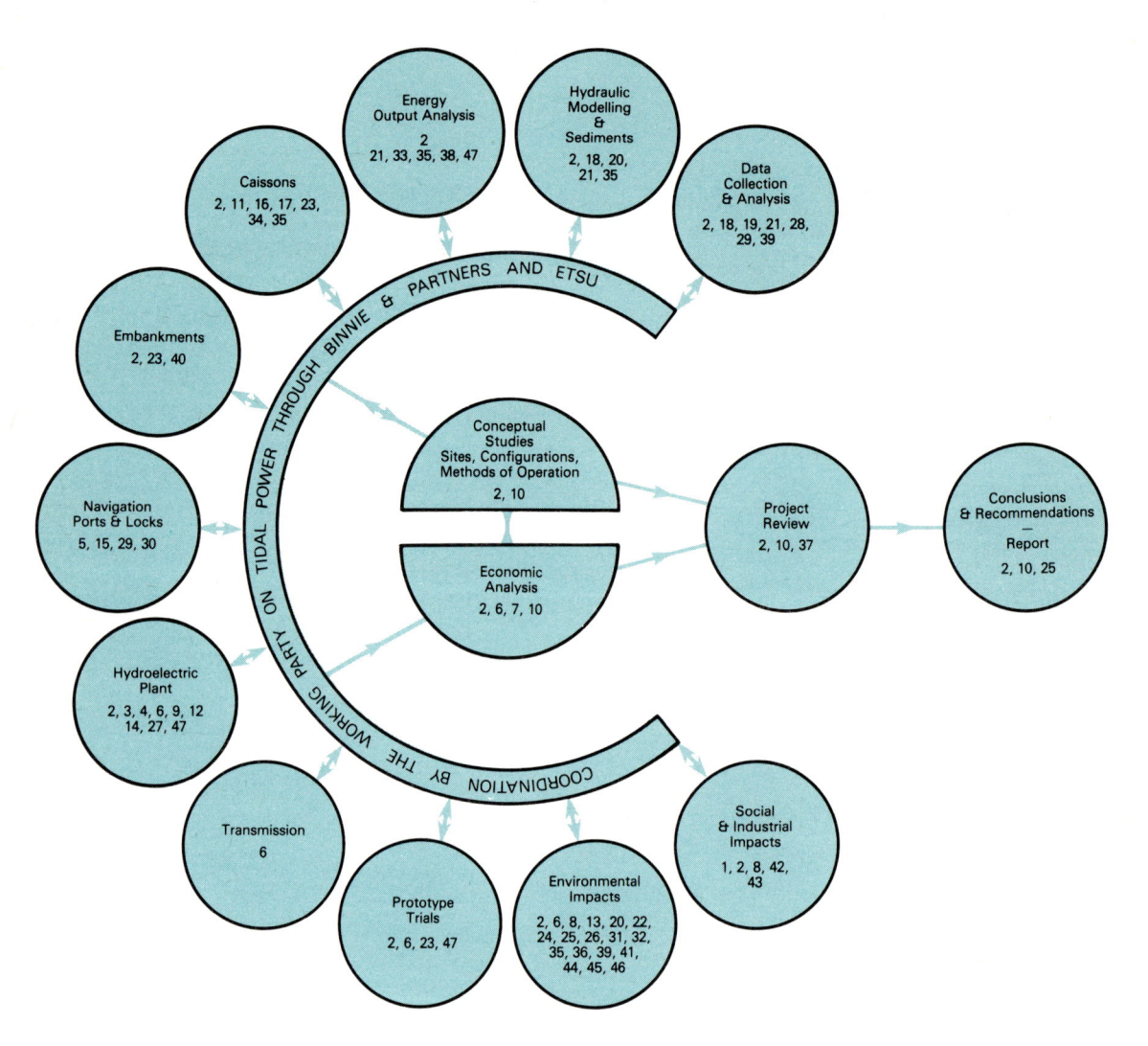

Caissons
2, 11, 16, 17, 23, 34, 35

Energy Output Analysis
2
21, 33, 35, 38, 47

Hydraulic Modelling & Sediments
2, 18, 20, 21, 35

Data Collection & Analysis
2, 18, 19, 21, 28, 29, 39

Embankments
2, 23, 40

Navigation Ports & Locks
5, 15, 29, 30

Hydroelectric Plant
2, 3, 4, 6, 9, 12, 14, 27, 47

Transmission
6

Prototype Trials
2, 6, 23, 47

Environmental Impacts
2, 6, 8, 13, 20, 22, 24, 25, 26, 31, 32, 35, 36, 39, 41, 44, 45, 46

Social & Industrial Impacts
1, 2, 8, 42, 43

Conceptual Studies Sites, Configurations, Methods of Operation
2, 10

Economic Analysis
2, 6, 7, 10

Project Review
2, 10, 37

Conclusions & Recommendations — Report
2, 10, 25

COORDINATION BY THE WORKING PARTY ON TIDAL POWER THROUGH BINNIE & PARTNERS AND ETSU

1. Atkins Planning
2. Binnie & Partners
3. Boving & Co. Ltd.
4. Boving/Escher Wyss Consortium
5. British Transport Docks Board
*6. Central Electricity Generating Board
*7. Department of Energy
*8. Department of the Environment
*9. Department of Industry
10. Energy Technology Support Unit
11. Engineering & Power Development Consultants Ltd
12. Escher Wyss
13. Field Studies Council
14. GEC Machines Ltd
15. Gloucester Harbour Trustees
16. J.H. Gordon, Consulting Eng.
17. Sir William Halcrow & Partners
18. Hydraulics Research Station
19. Institute of Geological Sciences (NERC)
20. Institute for Marine Environmental Research (NERC)
21. Institute of Oceanographic Sciences (NERC)
22. Institute of Terrestrial Ecology (NERC)
23. Sir Robert McAlpine & Sons Ltd
*24. Ministry of Agriculture, Fisheries & Food
*25. Natural Environment Research Council (NERC)
26. Nature Conservancy Council
27. Neyrpic
28. Pilots in Bristol Channel/Severn Estuary
29. Port of Bristol Authority
30. Rendel Palmer and Tritton
31. Sea Mammal Research Unit (NERC)
*32. Severn Trent Water Authority
33. Shawater Limited
34. Taywood Engineering Ltd
35. University of Bristol
36. University College, Cardiff
37. University of Manchester Institute of Science and Technology
38. University of Salford
39. University of Wales Institute of Science and Technology
40. Wallace Evans & Partners
41. Water Research Centre
*42. Water Space Amenity Commission
*43. Welsh Office
44. Welsh Water Authority
*45. Wessex Water Authority
*46. The Wildfowl Trust
47. Prof. E. M. Wilson

*non-contractor

ANNEX FOUR: ORGANISATION AND STRUCTURE OF THE STUDY

Organisation

1. The overall programme of pre-feasibility studies was made up of over 80 individual but closely inter-related items. These were carried out for the Department of Energy by a variety of organisations including civil, mechanical and electrical engineering contractors and consultants in industry, government laboratories including the Hydraulics Research Station and various NERC institutes, university departments etc. Environmental studies made use of knowledge and expertise in local universities as well as the experience of NERC institutes, the Nature Conservancy Council and the Central Electricity Generating Board.

2. The Committee gratefully acknowledges important contributions to the study made free of charge by the Central Electricity Generating Board and several regional Water Authorities.

3. The programme was subdivided into a number of subject areas (data, engineering, environmental etc), work in each of these areas being closely coordinated. Good coordination was a vital feature of the programme because of the highly interactive nature of the work. Progress was made via an interative procedure, as results from some studies were used to provide refined input data for other study areas.

4. Fig 49 shows a simplified flow chart illustrating the main subject areas in which work was carried out and the organisations involved in each of them.

Structure of the Study

Data Collection

5. A good data base was considered essential for this programme. For this reason, about a quarter of the funds have been spent on the following main items of data collection:

- a geophysical and geological survey, including some sediment sampling, of the whole of the Severn Estuary as far as a line between Nash Point and Porlock,
- wave measurements using buoys,
- temporary and long term tide gauging including offshore gauges in the outer estuary and on the Holm Islands,
- current velocities, suspended and mobile bottom sediment concentrations and salinity,
- surveys of wading birds and gulls, of intertidal, sublittoral and benthic fauna and of sites of special scientific or other interest.

6. Use was made of much existing data, for example that collected on water quality in the estuary and the sub-estuaries by the Water Authorities and the Institute of Marine Environmental Research and on fine sediments in the estuary by the Institute of Oceanographic Sciences.

Annex 4 (Continued)

Mathematical Models

7. Mathematical models have been used to simulate many aspects of barrage construction and performance. These have included:
- the construction phase, involving the progressive restriction of the tidal waterway as works are built and its influence on water levels and currents,
- scheme operation, to define energy outputs for a range of selected schemes and layouts, and to predict the effects of schemes on water levels and currents both inside and outside the barrage,
- a system study to evaluate the economic performance of tidal power schemes within the context of the CEGB's electricity generating system.

8. Three types of model of water movement have been used:
- flat surface models representing local effects at the barrage. These were mainly used to assess water velocities during barrage construction.
- one dimensional (1-D) models, in which the tidal dynamics of the estuary are represented in a simplified way by assuming that water flows are evenly spread over cross-sections at right-angles to the axis of the estuary,
- 2-D models in which the tidal propagation is represented through a grid of boxes of varying depths which represent the estuary. This type of model is 'vertically integrated' so does not differentiate between layers of flow, but can represent the different tides on the two shores of the estuary and include such effects as the Earth's rotation and wind stress.

9. The models are listed in order of increasing cost, the cost of a run in each succeeding model being about an order of magnitude greater than the previous type. Thus the first type of model has been used to compare a wide range of types and size of scheme and narrow down the range of parameters for subsequent testing by the second type, and so forth.

Engineering Studies

10. The engineering studies have proceeded on the basis of progressive refinement as data became available and as the number of schemes being studied was reduced. At the beginning of the study, preliminary outline designs were drawn up and costed, using 'all-in' rates, for the turbine caissons, sluice caissons, embankment and ship locks. For these, conservative assumptions were made regarding design criteria such as wave heights and ground strength. For the short-listed schemes, more detailed designs were prepared and costed.

11. In general a conservative engineering approach was adopted and for this reason most consideration was given to bulb turbines. However, the turbine runner diameter used as the reference case was 9m, this being considered a reasonable extrapolation of existing technology. Turbines of other types (tubular, rim generator) and smaller size (7½m diameter) were studied to determine their relative merits.

Economic Analysis

12. Initially the economic performance of various tidal power schemes was estimated by considering their crude generating costs in p/kWh. This enabled tidal power to be compared in broad terms with conventional power generation and a relative ranking of different tidal power schemes to be made. For the most promising schemes a fuller economic analysis was carried out using a modified version of the Department of Energy's investment model of the electricity generating system in England and Wales.

13. A risk and sensitivity analysis was then carried out to determine the sensitivity of conclusions on economic viability to uncertainties in, e.g. barrage construction time, cost, energy output and future value of energy.

Evaluation of Social and Industrial Impacts

14. The most immediate impact would be on ports behind a barrage. Effort was therefore concentrated on determining the locking requirements for the leading barrage schemes and the overall effect of a barrage on navigation and port access.

15. Broad consideration was given to other social and industrial impacts to identify their main features. However, no attempt was made to quantify many of these impacts, an exception being the potential recreational benefits.

Annex 4 (Continued)

Environmental Impact Assessment

16. A tidal power scheme would have wide-ranging and important impacts on nature, both adverse and beneficial. Early work concentrated on defining the sensitive issues for all schemes and on research items with a long lead time, e.g. studies on migratory fish. To avoid a great deal of wasted effort, impacts were only assessed in detail relatively late in the study programme for a few chosen barrage schemes. Although it is intrinsically not possible to place a financial value on certain environmental impacts, the costs of measures needed to maintain water quality, land drainage and sea defences were estimated.

17. The results of the many individual studies were then correlated and analysed to enable an overall view of the likely environmental effects of a tidal power scheme to be formed.

ANNEX FIVE: DEFINITION OF SCENARIOS

Plant Cost and Characteristics (all scenarios, all years)

	Capital Cost[a, b] (£/kW)	Plant Life (years)	Thermal Efficiency (%)
Nuclear	1320	25	36
Coal Fired	713	30	35
Oil Fired	627	30[c]	35.5
Gas Turbines	350	30	25
Coal Fired CHP[d]	792	30	25[d]

Fuel Costs

	Fuel Cost[a,g] (p/therm)[e]			
	2000	2010	2020	2030
Coal				
Scenario I, II & III	34.3	35.6	37.4	39.3
High Variant	45.9	47.5	49.6	52.1
Low Variant	29.7	30.8	31.9	33.0
Fuel Oil				
Scenarios I & II	57.4	59.4	61.9	64.9
Scenario III	66.1	82.8	95.8	105.6
Distillate Oil				
Scenarios I & II	74.6	80.5	85.1	87.0
Scenario III	79.1	97.2	111.9	123.3
Nuclear Fuel[f]				
Scenarios I & II	9.1	10.4	11.7	13.3
Scenario III	7.1	8.1	9.0	9.9

Discount Rate
A central discount rate of 5% was assumed, with variants of 3% and 7%.

Plant Mix
The above assumptions lead to forecasts by the system model of plant mixes for the various scenarios as shown in Fig 21 in the main text.

Notes:
(a) For consistency with the rest of this report, costs are shown in terms of the value of money in December 1980. These figures are 32% higher than when expressed in March 1979 money, which was the base used throughout the economic evaluation.

(b) Capital costs include interest during construction and for nuclear plant also include initial fuelling.

(c) Reduced to 20 years in Scenario III.

(d) Coal fired Combined Heat and Power plant is assumed to have an electrical efficiency of 25% and a heat efficiency of 50%.

(e) 9.48 therms = 1 GJ

Electrical Demand

	Demand (GW)			
	2000	2010	2020	2030
System Maximum Demand				
Scenarios I & II	60.2	71.0	80.4	89.8
Scenario III	53.7	58.7	63.7	68.7
Low Variant	50.6	55.5	68.4	80.8
Heat from CHP Schemes				
All Scenarios	5.3	10.6	15.8	21.1

Nuclear Availability

	Average Annual Availability
Scenarios I & II	70
Scenario III	64
Low Variant	60

Constraint on the Rate of Installation of Nuclear Plant

	Maximum Rate of Nuclear Plant Completion (GW/year) where this is economic		
	1980-1990	1990-2000	post 2000
Scenario I	0.25*	2.2	3.0
Scenario II	0.25*	1.0	1.0
Scenario III	0.25*	2.2	unconstrained

*presently under construction

(f) Fossil fuel replacement basis.

(g) For comparison, actual fuel costs in pence/therm in 1979/80 expressed in December 1980 money values were:

Coal (internationally traded)	15.7
Fuel Oil	19.7
Distillate Oil	31.2
Nuclear Fuel (AGR)	7.3

ANNEX SIX: CRITERIA FOR COMPARISON OF INVESTMENT IN TIDAL AND NUCLEAR POWER

1. The main economic criterion used in this report for comparing alternative investments is the benefit to cost ratio. The benefit B is the reduction in discounted system cost of the rest of the electricity supply system, while costs are made up of capital (C_{cap}) and operating (C_{op}) components.

2. However, there are two alternative benefit/cost criteria which may be considered, namely:

(i) $\dfrac{B - C_{op}}{C_{cap}}$;   (ii) $\dfrac{B}{C_{op} + C_{cap}}$

Ratio (i) is the one used in this report. This focusses on the net benefit per unit of investment in capital works and is more applicable if money for capital investment is the main constraint. This is a standard criterion for industrial investment, and is one which the CEGB commonly evaluates. This criterion is consistent with the main principle of minimising the total costs of meeting electricity demand and has the additional attraction of being less sensitive to assumptions about systems operation in the future.

3. An alternative formulation is to consider the gross benefit per unit of total cost committed, including capital and operating components (criterion (ii)). This may be more applicable if, at a national level, we are interested in the return on the total commitment of resources over the lifetime of the project. It can, however, be misleading since it is not necessarily consistent with system accounting principles.

4. Since the operating costs of a tidal power plant are very small, both ratios give essentially the same value. However, for nuclear power ratio (i) yields values which are consistently higher than ratio (ii), because nuclear operating costs are not negligible.

5. This means that the relative economic performances of tidal and nuclear power are closer using criterion (ii) than when using criterion (i). Nevertheless with the assumptions made either of these criteria shows nuclear power to be the more attractive investment.

Fig 50 Comparison of an Inner Barrage with Nuclear Power

	Inner Barrage		Additional Nuclear Power, 4 GW	
	$\dfrac{B - C_{op}}{C_{cap}} \simeq \dfrac{B}{C_{op} + C_{cap}}$		$\dfrac{B - C_{op}}{C_{cap}}$	$\dfrac{B}{C_{op} + C_{cap}}$
Scenario I	1.10		2.00	1.60
Scenario II	1.40		2.30	1.75
Scenario III	0.95		1.55	1.35
Scenario I — but with 3% discount rate	1.60		2.20	1.65
Scenario I — but with 7% discount rate	0.75		1.75	1.50
Scenario II — but with reduced availability of nuclear plant, (a).	1.40		1.85	1.55

(a) 60% average annual availability of nuclear plant, as compared with 70% in Scenarios I and II.

Note: Figures rounded to nearest 0.05

Fig 51 Estimates of Cost and Extractable Energy for the Major Renewable Sources of Electricity Generation

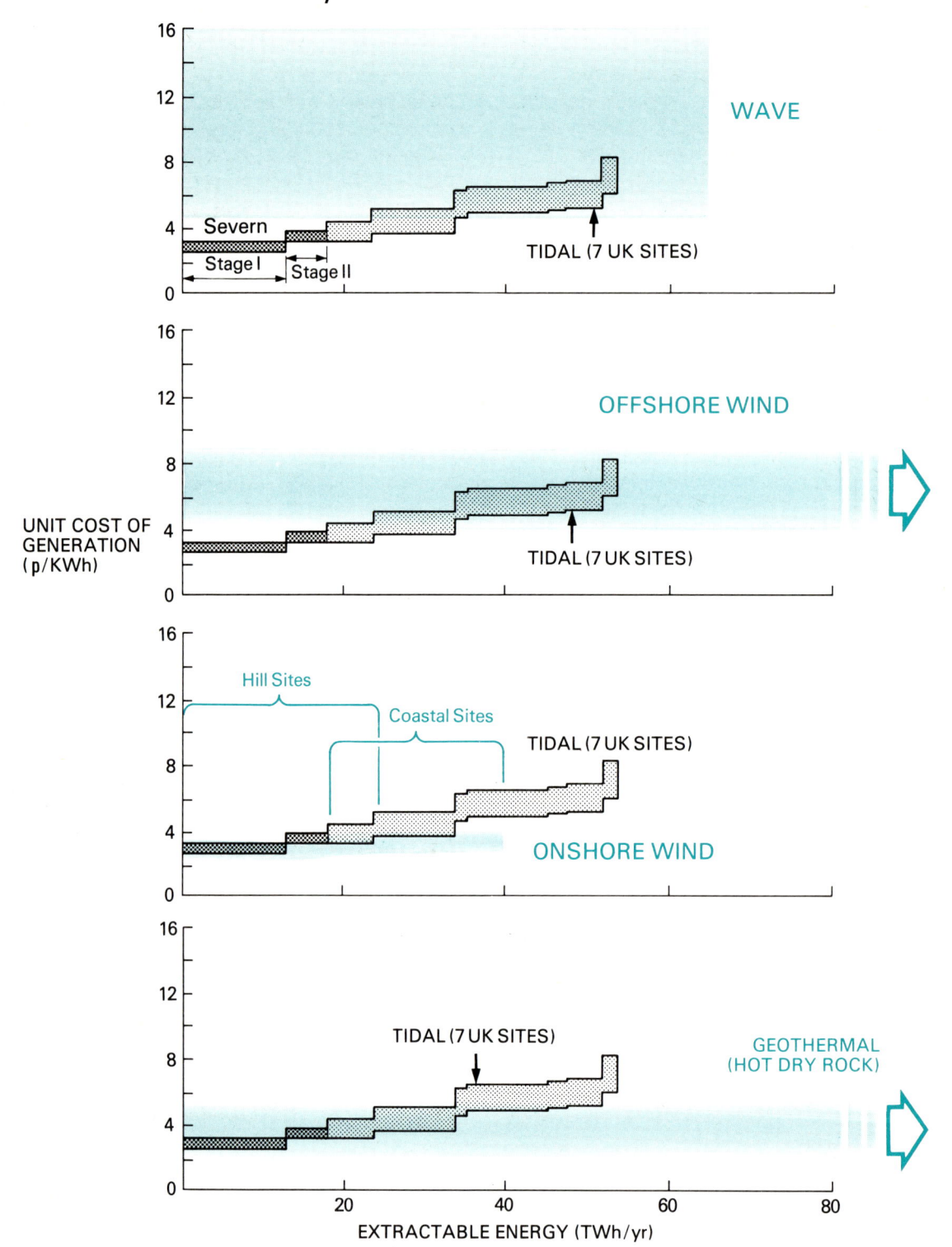

NOTES
1. Costs are expressed in December 1980 values.
2. Figures represent best estimates currently available from on-going Programmes.
3. Total UK power station supply is around 250 TWh/yr.
4. 1 TWh/yr represents about 0.4 mtce/yr in power station fuel.
5. These graphs illustrate the energy potentially extractable and do not necessarily imply that such amounts of energy could be fed into the grid.

ANNEX SEVEN: COMPARISON OF TIDAL POWER WITH OTHER RENEWABLE SOURCES OF ENERGY

1. The terms of reference of this initial study include the requirement to clarify the status of tidal power amongst the other renewable sources of energy. This is necessary if we are to be satisfied that no other new technology is likely to emerge in the short term which could invalidate our recommendation for substantial funding of further work towards a Severn Barrage.

2. In addition to tidal power, three other 'renewable' sources of electricity generation — wind, wave and geothermal (hot dry rock) are being actively researched under separate programmes funded by the Department of Energy. The technologies are discussed more fully in Volume 2. Any comparison of these energy sources requires three major factors to be taken into account; namely the extractable fraction of the UK resource, the likely cost and the state of technical development. Estimates of extractable energy and cost, based upon currently available data are shown in the figure opposite, although these may well be modified as the R&D programmes proceed. The least developed technologies (geothermal, wave, offshore wind) have the greatest potential for change in economic performance.

3. In order to derive an estimate of the total UK tidal power resource for the comparison, the methodology developed to assess energy outputs and likely costs has been applied to other estuaries. Seven sites including the Severn have been considered. Taken together these could provide about 54 TWh/yr, or about one quarter of the present UK electricity demand for 6-8p/kWh, while Stage I in the Severn (the Inner Barrage) could provide about 13 TWh/yr for around 3p/kWh. The derivation of estimates of extractable energy for the other renewables are summarised in Volume 2. These values, including those for tidal power in other estuaries, may be considerably reduced in practice by problems of environmental and social acceptability.

4. It should be noted that, in contrast with the other renewable sources of energy, tidal barrage power cannot easily be introduced in small modules, although the staged development proposed for the Severn Estuary remedies this to some extent. However, the resulting long lead time between the start of construction and commencement of generation is fully taken into account in the economic analysis.

5. The following major points arise from the comparison of the technologies:

- Only geothermal and land-based wind power have present cost estimates comparable with those for tidal power in the Severn.
- Tidal power has the ability, shared only by geothermal electricity, of being able to provide predictable output.
- Together with land-based wind power, tidal power is largely based on proven concepts and there is little need for fundamental development of technology. However, geothermal electricity, wave power and offshore wind power still require considerable technological development.

6. Present information therefore indicates that, with the possible exception of land-based wind power (for which the contribution might be severely limited by environmental objections not taken into account in the figure opposite), none of the technologies is as close to technical and economic viability on a large scale as tidal power. None is considered likely to develop so rapidly to the point of large scale deployment that the attractiveness of a Severn Barrage would be affected.

Fig 52 The La Rance Tidal Power Scheme

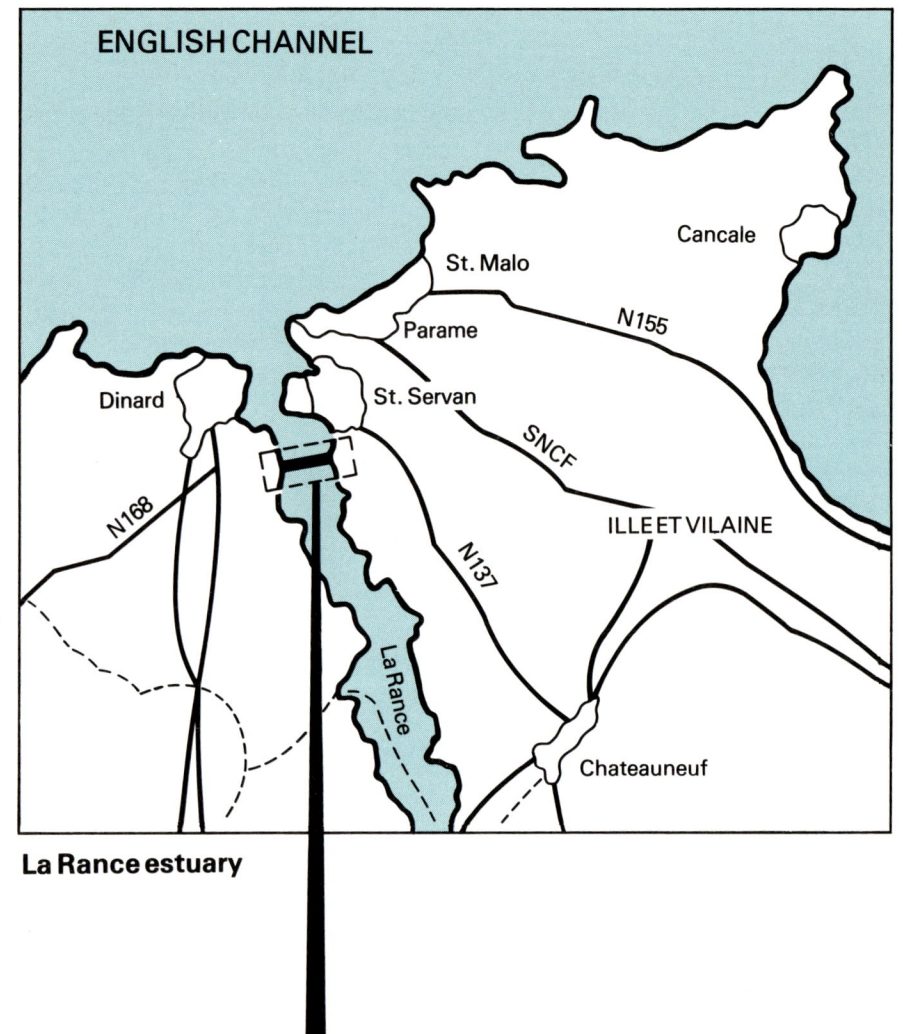

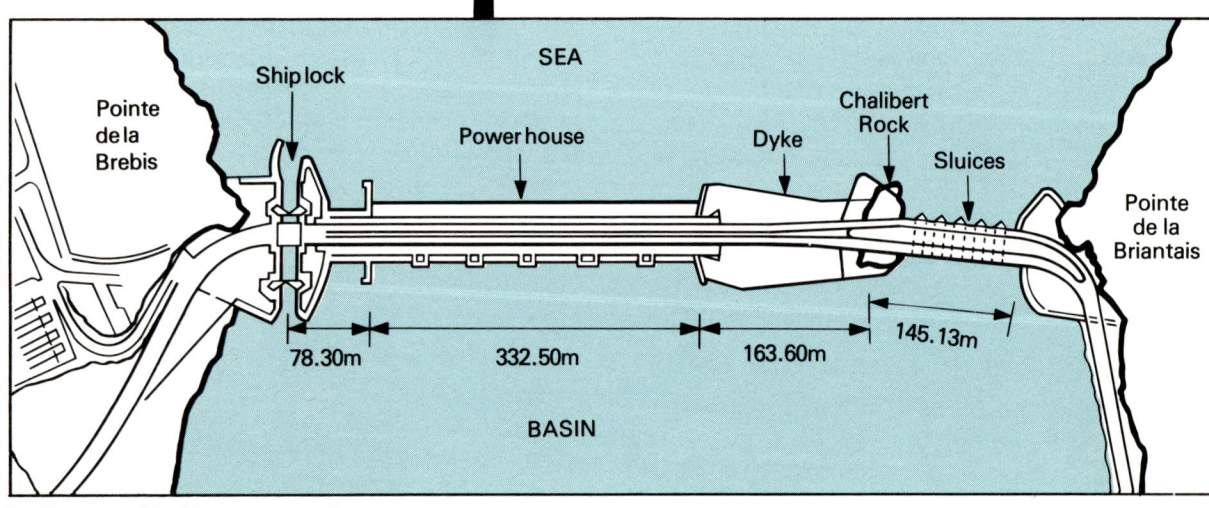

La Rance estuary

La Rance tidal barrage scheme

Scheme details
- Estuary width: 750 metres
- Basin area: 22 square kilometres
- Mean tide: 8.5 metres
- Installed generating power: 240 MW

- Turbo-generators: 24 × 10 MW bulb type Kaplan turbines with reverse flow and pumping capability
- Turbine runner diameter: 5.35 metres
- rated head: 5.65 metres
- maximum head: 11 metres
- minimum head: 3 metres

ANNEX EIGHT: VISIT BY THE SEVERN BARRAGE COMMITTEE TO THE LA RANCE BARRAGE 8th MAY 1980

Introduction

1. Apart from a very small scheme in Russia with a rating of 800 kW, the Rance scheme is the only operational tidal power scheme in the world. The Severn Barrage Committee visited the scheme and discussed its construction and operation so as to have a better understanding of the merits and problems of tidal power schemes.

2. The morning was spent discussing the history of La Rance. A film was shown of the construction of the scheme, including a previous prototype turbine installed in the lock entrance to a disused dock in St. Malo.

3. After lunch the Committee toured the barrage, spending most time in the turbine hall. This was followed by further technical discussion. The tidal cycle was at neaps with high tide in the afternoon so that the barrage was not working when toured.

Points noted

4. The Rance scheme was conceived as a large prototype to provide experience of the building and operation of a tidal plant in preparation for possible development of much larger schemes on the Brittany coast. For this reason, although only a single basin scheme, a design allowing for very flexible operation was chosen using combined double action pump turbines. Pumping can be used to augment the natural filling of the basin to achieve storage and increase output at peak load. Pumping can also lower the basin below sea level at low tide, again increasing peak load output. In addition it is possible to generate either single way, on the ebb only, or two-way on both ebb and flood. Although studies of tidal power have been dormant, interest is now reawakening in France for large single or two basin schemes with installed capacities up to 15,000 MW.

5. The Rance scheme was built between 1961 and 1967, the first energy being produced in 1966.

6. The turbine generators are double-regulated reversible machines, capable of turbining or pumping in each direction. Twenty four machines were installed, each 5.35m runner diameter with a 10 MW generator/motor. The total net electricity output is about 0.5 TWh/year, or 4% of an Inner Barrage in the Severn. The turbines have now been immersed for about 100,000 hours and have operated for up to 70,000 hours. The only major fault has been the failure of the lugs holding the generator stators in position in the bulb housings. This has been caused by the severe stresses arising during the start-up for pumping, which is 'direct on line'. Otherwise, problems have been confined to details such as the seals at the back of the runner hubs. The overall plant availability, excluding the problem with the fixing lugs, has been about 93%. By carrying out routine maintenance during neap tides, loss of energy is kept to a minimum and so energy availability has been about 96%.

7. At the time of the visit, four turbines were dismantled so the Committee were able to inspect the components of a bulb turbine at close quarters. A comprehensive impressed current cathodic protection system had been incorporated into the scheme. This uses about 20 kW and has been very successful in preventing corrosion of either the stainless steel runner blades and removable draft tube adjacent to the runner, or of the normal steel used for the bulbs, the built-in draft tube liner and the other submerged metal parts. A sophisticated paint system had been used on the normal steel components but this would not now be considered necessary. Stainless steel runner blades were awaiting re-assembly and appeared to be in virtually new condition. Twelve turbines had these, the other twelve having aluminium bronze blades. The refurbishing programme is based on three sets at a time being out of commission. Four sets were out at the time of the visit because one set had just been dismantled while another was due back in service in a day or so. Maintenance is carried out within the turbine hall, two gantry cranes being provided, each covering half the length of the hall and a central assembly/maintenance area. Fifty five staff are employed at La Rance on operation and maintenance.

8. The navigation lock was originally designed to accommodate a certain size of naval craft and was larger than required by other users, including some commercial barge traffic. In the event, the French navy had not had occasion to use the lock and commercial traffic was minimal. However, the use by pleasure craft of the lock was now so great that a larger lock would have been useful at peak times. No toll is charged, costs being paid for by EDF. No spare gates are kept and no damage has been sustained by the gates as a result of collision. The lock sill is 2m above minimum sea level so routine maintenance is simple.

9. The dual two-lane road along the top of the barrage is well used. The roads authority provided and maintain the road surface. The bridge over

Annex 8 (Continued)

the lock is a simple single span, opening by rotating upwards. Traffic is controlled by lights and drop barriers similar to those at railway level crossings.

10. With the benefit of hindsight, the hosts considered that there would be few changes in the design of the scheme if it were done again. Informally, the 160m length of embankment was considered unnecessary, more turbines being a better choice.

11. When generation starts a turbine can be brought up to synchronous speed in less than a minute. Thus all the turbines could be brought on line in parallel in less than two minutes. However, care has to be exercised over the rate at which the turbines and sluice gates are opened up or closed to avoid waves travelling up the estuary which could be dangerous to people at the water's edge. Operation is controlled locally but times of pumping and generation are scheduled by the regional office of EDF in accordance with the time and height of tide. The flexibility of the two-way generation capability enables the barrage to respond occasionally to unscheduled requests for energy.

12. The Committee's hosts were enthusiastic about the merits of pumping at high tide (at low head) to raise the basin water level. The pumped water, released at a higher head during generation, is claimed to produce a net energy gain. This does not agree with the results obtained in the Severn studies, possibly because the Rance scheme has proportionately a much smaller area of sluices.

13. If the Rance scheme were built today, using the same construction methods, it would cost 1500M francs* (about £160M). The unit cost of electricity produced, including interest and depreciation, would be 31 centimes* or about 3.3p/kWh. This is competitive with oil-fired power stations but about twice the cost of electricity from nuclear stations.

---

*Prices quoted by Electricité de France to the Committee during their visit in May 1980.

ANNEX NINE: GLOSSARY OF TERMS

This annex is divided into three parts: a glossary of terms, a list of abbreviations and a list of units.

GLOSSARY OF TERMS

Air Saturation Value is the amount of oxygen water would contain if it were in equilibrium with air.

Armouring of an embankment is the protection of its surface layers by e.g. rock or specially designed concrete units such as dolosse.

Availability of a power station is the ratio of the energy which it would produce if restricted only by plant faults and maintenance to that which it could produce if there were no limitations.

Avoidable Operating Costs are those operating costs which can be avoided when plant is not generating but on stand-by, e.g. fuel but not manpower.

Bascule Bridge is a lifting bridge, hinged at one end.

Benefit/Cost Ratio is defined in this report as the ratio of net discounted benefit arising from the barrage (i.e. the reduction in discounted cost of the rest of the electricity supply system) to the total discounted cost of barrage construction and maintenance. The ratio used (see Annex 6) is

$$\frac{\text{Benefits} - \text{Operating Costs}}{\text{Capital Costs}}$$

and *not*

$$\frac{\text{Benefits}}{\text{Capital Costs} + \text{Operating Costs}}$$

Biochemical Oxygen Demand is the amount of oxygen required for biochemical oxidation of organic and inorganic matter. Values used in this study are amounts required during five days of biochemical oxidation.

Blank (or Blind) Caisson is one with no openings for water flow. It may be used instead of embankment.

Bulb Turbine is a type of turbo-generator in which the generator is housed in a pod located in the centre of the turbine passageway.

Bund or Bunded Enclosure is a basin formed on the side of the estuary by a dam which starts and finishes on the same side of the estuary.

Caisson is a large prefabricated concrete structure which is floated into position and then sunk into place.

Capacity Contribution, or firm capacity, of a tidal power scheme is the total installed capacity of other generating plant which would otherwise need to be constructed to meet the same electrical power demand with the same system security.

Cavitation is the formation of vapour filled cavities in the water, for example in the turbine passageway, as a result of a local drop in pressure. Their subsequent collapse in regions of higher pressure, for example adjacent to solid surfaces such as the turbine blades, can in time cause pitting and disintegration.

Cill (Sill) of a lock is the structure immediately under the lock gate. In practical terms it is the highest point of the bottom of the lock.

Coliform Bacteria are a group derived from the intestinal tracts of man and other warm blooded animals. Their presence is used as an indicator of sewage pollution.

Conservative Pollutant is one having high stability and resistance to degradation. It behaves as if it is only affected by dilution and dispersion.

Conventional Power Stations, in the context of this report, are those which employ established technologies, e.g. coal, oil and nuclear stations.

Cycling of electricity generating plant is the term used to describe periodic running up and down of its output. For some types of plant this can result in penalties to thermal efficiency, maintenance requirements and plant lifetime.

Annex 9 (Continued)

Deposition refers to the process of accretion of sediments.

Dinorwic is a large modern high-head pumped storage scheme in North Wales. It is able to generate 1320 MW within 10 seconds of starting and has a maximum rating of over 1800 MW.

Discount Rate is that rate used in discounting all benefits and costs.

Discounting is a method of assessing the present worth of a stream of costs or benefits arising at various times in the future. The calculation is made in real terms and is not an allowance for inflation. It attempts to allow for the preference for money now rather than later.

Dispersion of pollutants is their spreading within a body of water. The rate at which this occurs is described by a dispersion coefficient.

Diversity of supply in an electricity generating system is a concept related to the number of types of generating plant and fuels used. With increased diversity the risk of failure to meet electricity demand, e.g. through plant type faults or fuel shortage, is reduced.

Double Regulated Turbine is one with two separate methods of regulating the water flow and hence power output, e.g. one with adjustable guide vanes (distributor) and runner blades.

Draft Tube is the turbine passageway downstream of the turbine runner. It is designed to maximise the amount of energy which can be extracted from the water by ensuring a rapid flow past the turbine runner but a minimum discharge velocity.

Earth Science Sites are sites of geological and geomorphological interest.

Ebb Generation is a mode of tidal power generation in which water passes through the turbines in the same direction as the ebb tide, i.e. from the basin to the sea.

Economic Investment is used in this report to mean one in which benefits exceed costs when discounted at a rate of 5% p.a. in real terms, which corresponds to the minimum 5% rate of return for public investment currently required by Treasury.

Ecosystem is a community of organisms and their environment.

Effective Length of an estuary is the length of the equivalent open straight sided channel having the same natural period of resonance.

Embankment is a mound, bank or section of a dam or dyke made from rock, sand and similar materials.

Energy Paper 23 "Tidal Power Barrages in the Severn Estuary", HMSO 1977.

Energy Paper 27 "Severn Barrage Seminar, September 7th, 1977", HMSO.

Energy Potential is used to describe the amount of energy which could theoretically be extracted from the tides at a given barrage site by using very large numbers of turbines.

Energy Projections 1979 is an energy forecast published by the Department of Energy.

Energy Storage — see **Storage**.

Environment is frequently used in this report in the widest sense, including the social and industrial aspects of man's environment.

Erosion is the process of removal of sediments from an existing deposit.

Exposure of geological sites is where the geological strata reach the surface.

Firm Capacity — see capacity contribution.

Annex 9 (Continued)

Fish Pass is a structure designed to enable fish to pass a barrier.

Flap Gate is a type of sluice gate as illustrated in Fig 7.

Flood Generation is a mode of tidal power operation in which water passes through the turbines in the same direction as the flood tide, i.e. from the sea to the basin.

Foreshore is the zone between low water and high water.

Geomorphology is the science of the shape of landforms, including those under the sea.

Generator Rating, or rated electrical output, is the normal maximum output.

Geothermal Energy is energy obtained from heat within the Earth.

Habitat is the normal abode or locality of an animal or plant.

Head of water driving a tidal power turbine is the difference in levels between the basin and the sea. This is the primary factor determining the maximum power output of a turbine.

Heavy Metals are metals of higher atomic weight than iron. Some, like cadmium, are harmful to animals.

Hettangian Stage of the Lower Jurassic is represented in the Severn area by alternating thin limestones and shaly mudstones.

Internationally Traded Coal Price is the price of coal for power generation on the open world market.

Intertidal Area is the zone between low water and high water.

Jurassic is the middle division of Mesozoic rocks about 180 million years old. The Mesozoic is the geological period corresponding to the age of reptiles and includes the Triassic, Jurassic and Cretaceous.

La Rance Barrage in France is the only full scale tidal power scheme in the world. It is described briefly in Annex 8. However, a Severn Barrage could have an installed capacity some 30-60 times greater.

Lead Time is the time between initiation and completion of a study or a production process.

Load Factor is the ratio of the actual amount of energy produced by a power station to the maximum energy it would produce if running at full load all the time.

Longitudinal Dispersion is dispersion along the length, or axis of a river or estuary.

Lower Jurassic is the early part of the Jurassic period (see **Jurassic**)

Low-Head is a head of only a few metres, as in a tidal scheme. This may be compared with high heads of tens or hundreds of metres in hydro-electric and pumped storage schemes.

Mathematical Model is used synonomously with numerical model.

Man-Year is effort equivalent to one man working for one year. It could, of course, be made up of two men's work for six months each, etc.

Marginal Cost of Energy is the cost of an additional unit of energy, which could be obtained by adding an extra turbine or sluice, etc.

Marginal Vegetation is that vegetation along the estuary margin.

Marginal Wetland is that wetland along or close to the estuary margin.

Annex 9 (Continued)

Merit Order is a list of plant in ascending order of avoidable operating cost.

Migratory Fish are those whose life cycle involves migration between river and sea. In the Severn Estuary the known migratory species are salmon, sea-trout, allis-shad, twaite-shad and eel. Sea and river lamprey also migrate.

Multiplier Effect is a term used to describe the phenomenon whereby the wealth injected into the community as a result of a large project indirectly leads to new jobs in the locality other than those resulting directly from the project.

Neap Tides are the tides of lowest range in the spring-neap cycle. They occur when the Sun's gravitational field is acting at right angles to that of the Moon.

Net Operating Savings is the net reduction in system operating costs made by a particular plant.

Net Present Value is the net amount of the discounted future costs and revenues expressed in real terms associated with a capital investment.

Numerical Model is a computer based simulation of a real situation. In the case of the numerical hydrodynamic models used in this study, the equations of motion and continuity are solved in one or two dimensions.

Opportunity Cost of Capital is the real cost of using capital in terms of the opportunity foregone of using it elsewhere.

Orthophosphate in water quality terms is a chemical which acts as an algal nutrient. About 60% of this enters the estuary from point sources which are potentially controllable.

Oxygen-Demanding Substances are those which remove dissolved oxygen from the water if it is available.

Oxygen Transfer Efficiency is the efficiency of transfer of oxygen from the air to the water.

Post-Tender Design Change is a change made after the tender has been accepted for a job. Such changes commonly lead to increased costs.

Productivity of Organisms is the rate of production of new biomass.

Prototype Trial is a test of a component at full-scale, with the object of either proving a technology, or eliminating type faults, or refining cost estimates.

Radial Gate is a type of sluice gate, as illustrated in Fig 7.

Ramsar Convention was a convention on 'Wetlands of International Importance especially as Wildfowl Habitats' held at Ramsar in Iran in 1971. The 'International Conference on the Conservation of Wetlands and Waterfowl' held at Heilingenhafen in 1974 set down criteria for sites of international importance, e.g. a site that supports more than 20,000 waders is considered internationally important.

"Ramsar" Site is a site designated under the terms of the Ramsar Convention.

Real Terms means assuming constant money values, i.e. neglecting the effect of general inflation.

Renewable Sources of Energy is a generic term used to describe sources of energy which do not depend on a finite fuel resource. Examples are tidal, solar, wind and wave energy. For convenience, geothermal energy is often called a renewable source although strictly it is not.

Required Rate of Return is the minimum rate of return for investment. In the public sector this is currently set by Treasury at 5% in real terms (Cmnd. 7131, March 1978).

Resonance is enhanced amplification of a tide, the frequency of which is close to the natural frequency of oscillation of water in an estuary.

Annex 9 (Continued)

Residual Demand is the demand on the rest of the CEGB system once the output of the tidal power scheme has been subtracted from the total demand.

Reversible Turbine is one which is able to generate with a flow in either direction.

Rim Generator is a type in which the generator rotor is attached to the tips of the runner blades and the stator is in a dry housing surrounding the turbine.

Rockfill comprises pieces of rock used in the construction of embankments.

Runner is the rotating part of a turbine which converts the energy of flowing water into mechanical energy for driving a generator.

"Run-of-River" power scheme is a river hydro-electric scheme having little or no reservoir storage. Low heads of water are created by suitably placed dams.

Saline Intrusion is the intrusion of salt water into fresh water areas.

Salinity is a measure of the amount of salt in water.

Saltmarsh is the intertidal zone on sandy mud in sheltered coastal areas and estuaries, supporting salt tolerant plant communities. In the Severn area, the saltmarshes are mainly located in the central reaches of the estuary, on both sides of the channel, flanked by wide intertidal mud flats. Their total area is 1400 ha, fringing river mouths, e.g. the Usk and Parrett, and low-lying sheltered coasts, e.g. Clevedon.

Sand-Fill is sand used as fill material, e.g. for the core of an embankment as is shown in Fig 8.

Sand Island is an artificial island constructed mainly of dredged sand.

Scenario is a consistent and plausible view of the future, not a prediction or forecast or goal. A number of parameters are specified in a consistent manner.

Scour is rapid erosion of the estuary bed arising from high water velocities.

Sediment Transport is the process of movement of sediment by water.

Semi-Diurnal Cycle is a cycle repeated twice in a day.

Sludge refers to sewage sludge and is the solid or semi-solid residue of sewage treatment.

Sluice is a waterway in which the passage of water is controlled by gates.

Sluice Caisson is a caisson designed to include sluices.

Smolt are 2-4 year old salmon which have not yet gone to sea but are about to migrate.

Spartina is a salt tolerant grass. It has the ability to colonise intertidal flats and consolidate marshes which are subject to erosion.

Spring Tides are the tides of greatest range in the spring-neap cycle. They occur at or near new and full Moon when the solar and lunar gravitational fields reinforce each other.

Spring-Neap Cycle is the 14-day periodic cycle of tides. This is due to occurrance of maxima and minima in the combined effects of the Sun's and Moon's gravitational fields.

Annex 9 (Continued)

Storage The purposes of energy storage within an electricity generating system is described in Fig 17.

Substratum is the surface to which an organism is attached or upon which it moves.

Sub-tidal Habitat is one which is permanently inundated by the tide.

Synchronised The output of a turbo-generator is said to be synchronised with the grid when the wave form of its alternating electrical output is locked in phase with the grid.

System Cost is the total cost of meeting electricity demand and is the sum of various cost elements, such as capital, fuel, maintenance, overheads etc.

Systems Model in the context of this report is a computerised investment model of the CEGB's electricity generating system.

System Security refers to the degree of assurance with which the generating system can meet the winter peak in electrical demand. Such assurance is obtained by installing generating plant with a total rated capacity in excess of this peak to allow for plant availability in winter, load estimating errors and weather of unusual severity.

Thermal Power Station is a power station in which primary energy (coal, oil, nuclear) is converted to heat to form steam to drive turbines, for electricity generation.

Tidal Range is the difference in water levels between high water and low water.

Total Inorganic Nitrogen is made up of nitrogen as nitrate, nitrite and ammonia. It is an algal nutrient and, in the Severn Estuary, mostly arises from diffuse sources which are not potentially controllable.

Tubular Turbine is a type of turbine in which power take-off is via a long shaft coupled to a gearbox, enabling a high-speed generator to be used.

Turbidity is a measure of the clarity of water from which the amount of suspended solids in the water may be inferred.

Turbine Caisson is a caisson designed to carry one or more turbines.

Turbine Runner — see **Runner**.

Turbo-Generator is a turbine coupled to a generator.

Two-way Generation is a mode of tidal power generation on both the ebb and flood tides.

Vertical Lift Gate is one which lifts vertically in opening and closing sluice passageways, as illustrated in Fig 7.

Wader is a wading bird.

Water Table is the level below which all fissures and pores in the ground are filled with water.

Wave Attack is the process of waves attacking and eroding or damaging structures.

Wave Cut Platform is a platform formed by the action of waves on a rock surface.

Wetland is an area of relatively poorly drained land with its characteristic ecosystem.

LIST OF ABBREVIATIONS

a.c.	— alternating current
CEGB	— Central Electricity Generating Board
d.c.	— direct current
EEC	— European Economic Community

Annex 9 (Continued)

GCR	— A Geological Conservation Review, NCC, *in preparation*	kilo	**symbol k** meaning 10^3
HWOST	— High Water Ordinary Spring Tide	micro	**symbol μ** meaning 10^{-6}

billion is used to mean one thousand million
and the following abbreviations are used: —

LWOST — Low Water Ordinary Spring Tide	
NCC — Nature Conservancy Council	
NCR — A Nature Conservation Review, Radcliffe, D.A. (Ed) NCC and NERC, 1977	
NERC — Natural Environment Research Council	
NNR — National Nature Reserve	
O.D. — Ordnance Datum	
SSSI — Site of Special Scientific Interest	

dwt	dead weight tons (ships' carrying capacity)
GJ	gigajoule
GW	gigawatt
ha	hectare (10,000m^2)
km	kilometre
kV	kilovolt
kWh	kilowatt-hour
m	metre
mtce	million tonnes of coal equivalent
MW	megawatt
p	pence
p/kWh	pence per kilowatt-hour
TWh	terrawatt-hour
£k	thousands of pounds
£M	millions of pounds
μg/l	micro-grammes per litre

UNITS

The following prefixes are used for multiples of units: —

tera	**symbol T** meaning 10^{12}
giga	**symbol G** meaning 10^{9}
mega	**symbol M** meaning 10^{6}

1 therm = 0.1055 GJ
1 p/therm = 9.49 p/GJ

111

Printed in England for Her Majesty's Stationery Office by Commercial Colour Press, London E.7.
Dd.0716595 C30 5/81 CCP